The Shopkeeper Turned Gentleman

Moliere (Poquelin)

The Shopkeeper Turned Gentleman

Table of Contents

The Shopkeeper Turned Gentleman..1
   Moliere (Poquelin)..1
ACT I..5
      SCENE I.—MUSIC MASTER, DANCING MASTER, THREE SINGERS, TWO VIOLIN PLAYERS, FOUR DANCERS..5
      SCENE II.—MR. JOURDAIN (in a dressing-gown and night-cap), THE MUSIC MASTER, THE DANCING MASTER, THE PUPIL OF THE MUSIC MASTER, A LADY SINGER, TWO MEN SINGERS, DANCERS, TWO SERVANTS..7
ACT II..14
      SCENE I.—MR. JOURDAIN, DANCING MASTER, MUSIC MASTER..................15
      SCENE II.—MR. JOURDAIN, MUSIC MASTER, DANCING MASTER, A SERVANT..17
      SCENE III.—MR. JOURDAIN, FENCING MASTER, MUSIC MASTER, DANCING MASTER, A SERVANT holding two foils..17
      SCENE IV.—PROFESSOR OF PHILOSOPHY, MR. JOURDAIN, MUSIC MASTER, DANCING MASTER, FENCING MASTER, A SERVANT..........20
      SCENE V.—MR. JOURDAIN, A SERVANT..22
      SCENE VI.—PROFESSOR OF PHILOSOPHY, MR. JOURDAIN, A SERVANT..22
      SCENE VII.—MR. JOURDAIN, A SERVANT...28
      SCENE VIII.—MR. JOURDAIN, THE MASTER TAILOR, AN ASSISTANT TAILOR (bringing a suit of clothes for MR. JOURDAIN), A SERVANT..29
      SCENE IX.—MR. JOURDAIN, MASTER TAILOR, ASSISTANT TAILORS (dancing), A SERVANT..31
ACT III..32
      SCENE I.—MR. JOURDAIN, TWO LACKEYS..32
      SCENE II.—MR. JOURDAIN, NICOLE, TWO LACKEYS..........................32
      SCENE III.—MRS. JOURDAIN, MR. JOURDAIN, NICOLE, TWO SERVANTS..35
      SCENE IV.—DORANTE, MR. JOURDAIN, MRS. JOURDAIN, NICOLE.....41
      SCENE V.—DORANTE, MRS. JOURDAIN, NICOLE..................................45
      SCENE VI.—MR. JOURDAIN, MRS. JOURDAIN, DORANTE, NICOLE......46
      SCENE VII.—MRS. JOURDAIN, NICOLE..49

The Shopkeeper Turned Gentleman

Table of Contents

The Shopkeeper Turned Gentleman
    SCENE VIII.—NICOLE, CLEONTE, COVIELLE..................................49
    SCENE IX.—CLEONTE, COVIELLE...50
    SCENE X.—LUCILE, CLEONTE, COVIELLE, NICOLE.......................53
    SCENE XI.—MRS. JOURDAIN, CLEONTE, LUCILE, COVIELLE, NICOLE..59
    SCENE XII.—CLEONTE, MR. JOURDAIN, MRS. JOURDAIN, LUCILE, COVIELLE, NICOLE...60
    SCENE XIII.—MRS. JOURDAIN, LUCILE, CLEONTE, NICOLE, COVIELLE..62
    SCENE XIV.—CLEONTE, COVIELLE..62
    SCENE XV.—MR. JOURDAIN (alone)..63
    SCENE XVI.—MR. JOURDAIN, A SERVANT....................................63
    SCENE XVII—DORIMENE, DORANTE, A SERVANT.......................64
    SCENE XVIII.—DORIMENE, DORANTE..64
    SCENE XIX.—MR. JOURDAIN, DORIMENE, DORANTE..................65
    SCENE XX.—MR. JOURDAIN, DORIMENE, DORANTE, A SERVANT.....67
    SCENE XXI.—Entry of the BALLET..67
ACT IV..67
    SCENE I.—DORIMENE, MR. JOURDAIN, DORANTE, THREE SINGERS, A SERVANT...67
    SCENE II.—MRS. JOURDAIN, MR. JOURDAIN, DORIMENE, DORANTE, SINGERS, SERVANTS...70
    SCENE III.—MRS. JOURDAIN, MR. JOURDAIN, A SERVANT..........71
    SCENE IV.—MR. JOURDAIN (alone)..72
    SCENE V.—MR. JOURDAIN, COVIELLE (disguised).......................72
    SCENE VI.—CLEONTE (dressed as a Turk), THREE PAGES (carrying the vest of CLEONTE), MR. JOURDAIN, COVIELLE.........................76
    SCENE VII.—COVIELLE (alone)..77
    SCENE VIII.—DORANTE, COVIELLE..77
    SCENE IX.—THE TURKISH CEREMONY. [Footnote: Lulli composed the music, and acted the part of the Mufti.]..78
    SCENE X.—THE MUFTI, DERVISH, TURKISH SINGERS and DANCERS. MR. JOURDAIN, dressed like a Turk, his head shaved, without any turban or sword...78

The Shopkeeper Turned Gentleman

Table of Contents

The Shopkeeper Turned Gentleman
    SCENE XI.—THE MUFTI, DERVISHES, TURKS, singing and dancing.........79
    SCENE XI.—TURKS, singing and dancing. Second entry of the BALLET......81
    SCENE XIII.—THE MUFTI, DERVISHES, MR. JOURDAIN, TURKS, singing and dancing..81
ACT V..83
    SCENE I.—MRS. JOURDAIN, MR. JOURDAIN...83
    SCENE II.—DORANTE, DORIMENE..85
    SCENE III.—MR. JOURDAIN, DORIMENE, DORANTE...............................86
    SCENE IV.—MR. JOURDAIN, DORIMENE, DORANTE, CLEONTE (dressed as a Turk)..87
    SCENE V.—MR. JOURDAIN, DORIMENE, DORANTE, CLEONTE (dressed as a Turk); COVIELLE (disguised)...87
    SCENE VI.—LUCILE, CLEONTE, MR. JOURDAIN, DORIMENE, DORANTE, COVIELLE..88
    SCENE VII.—MRS. JOURDAIN. CLEONTE, MR. JOURDAIN, LUCILE, DORANTE, DORIMENE, COVIELLE..89

The Shopkeeper Turned Gentleman

Moliere (Poquelin)

Kessinger Publishing reprints thousands of hard-to-find books!

Visit us at http://www.kessinger.net

- ACT I.

  - SCENE I.—MUSIC MASTER, DANCING MASTER, THREE SINGERS, TWO VIOLIN PLAYERS, FOUR DANCERS.
  - SCENE II.—MR. JOURDAIN (in a dressing-gown and night-cap), THE MUSIC MASTER, THE DANCING MASTER, THE PUPIL OF THE MUSIC MASTER, A LADY SINGER, TWO MEN SINGERS, DANCERS, TWO SERVANTS.

- ACT II.

  - SCENE I.—MR. JOURDAIN, DANCING MASTER, MUSIC MASTER.
  - SCENE II.—MR. JOURDAIN, MUSIC MASTER, DANCING MASTER, A SERVANT.
  - SCENE III.—MR. JOURDAIN, FENCING MASTER, MUSIC MASTER, DANCING MASTER, A SERVANT holding two foils.
  - SCENE IV.—PROFESSOR OF PHILOSOPHY, MR. JOURDAIN, MUSIC MASTER, DANCING MASTER, FENCING MASTER, A SERVANT.
  - SCENE V.—MR. JOURDAIN, A SERVANT.
  - SCENE VI.—PROFESSOR OF PHILOSOPHY, MR. JOURDAIN, A SERVANT.
  - SCENE VII.—MR. JOURDAIN, A SERVANT.
  - SCENE VIII.—MR. JOURDAIN, THE MASTER TAILOR, AN ASSISTANT TAILOR (bringing a suit of clothes for MR. JOURDAIN), A SERVANT.
  - SCENE IX.—MR. JOURDAIN, MASTER TAILOR, ASSISTANT TAILORS (dancing), A SERVANT.

The Shopkeeper Turned Gentleman

- ACT III.

    - SCENE I.—MR. JOURDAIN, TWO LACKEYS.
    - SCENE II.—MR. JOURDAIN, NICOLE, TWO LACKEYS.
    - SCENE III.—MRS. JOURDAIN, MR. JOURDAIN, NICOLE, TWO SERVANTS.
    - SCENE IV.—DORANTE, MR. JOURDAIN, MRS. JOURDAIN, NICOLE.
    - SCENE V.—DORANTE, MRS. JOURDAIN, NICOLE.
    - SCENE VI.—MR. JOURDAIN, MRS. JOURDAIN, DORANTE, NICOLE.
    - SCENE VII.—MRS. JOURDAIN, NICOLE.
    - SCENE VIII.—NICOLE, CLEONTE, COVIELLE.
    - SCENE IX.—CLEONTE, COVIELLE.
    - SCENE X.—LUCILE, CLEONTE, COVIELLE, NICOLE.
    - SCENE XI.—MRS. JOURDAIN, CLEONTE, LUCILE, COVIELLE, NICOLE.
    - SCENE XII.—CLEONTE, MR. JOURDAIN, MRS. JOURDAIN, LUCILE, COVIELLE, NICOLE.
    - SCENE XIII.—MRS. JOURDAIN, LUCILE, CLEONTE, NICOLE, COVIELLE.
    - SCENE XIV.—CLEONTE, COVIELLE.
    - SCENE XV.—MR. JOURDAIN (alone).
    - SCENE XVI.—MR. JOURDAIN, A SERVANT.
    - SCENE XVII—DORIMENE, DORANTE, A SERVANT.
    - SCENE XVIII.—DORIMENE, DORANTE.
    - SCENE XIX.—MR. JOURDAIN, DORIMENE, DORANTE.
    - SCENE XX.—MR. JOURDAIN, DORIMENE, DORANTE, A SERVANT.
    - SCENE XXI.—Entry of the BALLET.

- ACT IV.

    - SCENE I.—DORIMENE, MR. JOURDAIN, DORANTE, THREE SINGERS, A SERVANT.
    - SCENE II.—MRS. JOURDAIN, MR. JOURDAIN, DORIMENE, DORANTE, SINGERS, SERVANTS.
    - SCENE III.—MRS. JOURDAIN, MR. JOURDAIN, A SERVANT.
    - SCENE IV.—MR. JOURDAIN (alone).
    - SCENE V.—MR. JOURDAIN, COVIELLE (disguised).

- SCENE VI.—CLEONTE (dressed as a Turk), THREE PAGES (carrying the vest of CLEONTE), MR. JOURDAIN, COVIELLE.
- SCENE VII.—COVIELLE (alone).
- SCENE VIII.—DORANTE, COVIELLE.
- SCENE IX.—THE TURKISH CEREMONY. [Footnote: Lulli composed the music, and acted the part of the Mufti.]
- SCENE X.—THE MUFTI, DERVISH, TURKISH SINGERS and DANCERS. MR. JOURDAIN, dressed like a Turk, his head shaved, without any turban or sword.
- SCENE XI.—THE MUFTI, DERVISHES, TURKS, singing and dancing.
- SCENE XI.—TURKS, singing and dancing. Second entry of the BALLET.
- SCENE XIII.—THE MUFTI, DERVISHES, MR. JOURDAIN, TURKS, singing and dancing.

- ACT V.

  - SCENE I.—MRS. JOURDAIN, MR. JOURDAIN.
  - SCENE II.—DORANTE, DORIMENE.
  - SCENE III.—MR. JOURDAIN, DORIMENE, DORANTE.
  - SCENE IV.—MR. JOURDAIN, DORIMENE, DORANTE, CLEONTE (dressed as a Turk).
  - SCENE V.—MR. JOURDAIN, DORIMENE, DORANTE, CLEONTE (dressed as a Turk); COVIELLE (disguised).
  - SCENE VI.—LUCILE, CLEONTE, MR. JOURDAIN, DORIMENE, DORANTE, COVIELLE.
  - SCENE VII.—MRS. JOURDAIN. CLEONTE, MR. JOURDAIN, LUCILE, DORANTE, DORIMENE, COVIELLE.

THE SHOPKEEPER TURNED GENTLEMAN. (LE BOURGEOIS GENTILHOMME.)

BY

The Shopkeeper Turned Gentleman

MOLIERE,

TRANSLATED INTO ENGLISH PROSE.

WITH SHORT INTRODUCTIONS AND EXPLANATORY NOTES.

BY

CHARLES HERON WALL.

'Le Bourgeois Gentilhomme' was acted before the King for the first time at Chambord, on October 14, 1670, and on November 28 at the Palais Royal. After the second representation, Louis XIV. said to Moliere, "You have never written anything which amused me more, and your play is excellent." But it obtained a still greater success in Paris, where the *bourgeois* willingly and good-humouredly laughed at what they deemed their neighbours' weaknesses. The three first acts are the best; Louis XIV. hurried Moliere so with the last that they degenerated into burlesque.

Moliere acted the part of the Bourgeois.

PERSONS REPRESENTED.

MR. JOURDAIN.

CLEONTE, *in love with* LUCILE.

DORANTE, *a count, in love with* DORIMENE.

COVIELLE, *servant to* CLEONTE.

A MUSIC MASTER, ETC.

A DANCING MASTER, ETC.

A FENCING MASTER.

The Shopkeeper Turned Gentleman

A PROFESSOR OF PHILOSOPHY.

A MASTER TAILOR.

ASSISTANT TAILORS.

TWO LACKEYS.

MRS. JOURDAIN.

LUCILE, *daughter to* MR. JOURDAIN.

DORIMENE, *a marchioness*.

NICOLE, *maid-servant to* MR. JOURDAIN.

The scene is in PARIS, *in* MR. JOURDAIN'S *house*.

THE SHOPKEEPER TURNED GENTLEMAN.

ACT I.

The overture is played by a great many instruments; and in the middle of the stage the PUPIL of the MUSIC MASTER is seated at a table composing a serenade which MR. JOURDAIN has asked for.

SCENE I.—MUSIC MASTER, DANCING MASTER, THREE SINGERS, TWO VIOLIN PLAYERS, FOUR DANCERS.

MUS. MAS. (*to the* MUSICIANS). Come into this room, and rest till he comes.

DAN. MAS. (*to the* DANCERS). Come also, on this side.

MUS. MAS. (*to his* PUPIL). Have you finished?

The Shopkeeper Turned Gentleman

PUP. Yes.

MUS. MAS. Let me see. Very good.

DAN. MAS. Is it anything new?

MUS. MAS. Yes; it is an air for a serenade that I made him compose while we are waiting for our gentleman to wake up.

DAN. MAS. Will you allow me to see what it is?

MUS. MAS. You shall hear it, as well as the dialogue, when he comes; he won't be long.

DAN. MAS. We both have plenty to do now; have we not?

MUS. MAS. Indeed we have. We have found the very man we both wanted. He brings us in a comfortable little income, with his notions of gentility and gallantry which he has taken into his head; and it would be well for your dancing and my music if everybody were like him.

DAN. MAS. No; not altogether. I wish, for his sake, that he would appreciate better than he does the things we give him.

MUS. MAS. He certainly understands them but little; but he pays well, and that is nowadays what our arts require above all things.

DAN. MAS. I must confess, for my part, that I rather hunger after glory. Applause finds a very ready answer in my heart, and I think it mortifying enough that in the fine arts we should have to exhibit ourselves before fools, and submit our compositions to the vulgar taste of an ass. No! say what you will, there is a real pleasure in working for people who are able to appreciate the refinements of an art; who know how to yield a kind recognition to the beauties of a work, and who, by felicitous approbations, reward you for your labour. Yes! the most charming recompense one can receive for the things which one does is to see them understood, and to have them received with the applause that honours. Nothing, in my opinion, can repay us better than this for all our fatigues; and the praises of the enlightened are a true delight to me.

MUS. MAS. I grant it; and I relish them as much as you do. There is certainly nothing more refreshing than the applause you speak of; still we cannot live on this flattering acknowledgment of our talent. Undiluted praise does not give competence to a man; we must have something more solid to fall back upon, and the best praise is the praise of the pocket. Our man, it is true, is a man of very limited capacity, who speaks at random upon all things, and only gives applause in the wrong place; but his money makes up for the errors of his judgment. He keeps his discernment in his purse, and his praises are golden. This ignorant, commonplace citizen is, as you see, better to us than that clever nobleman who introduced us here.

DAN. MAS. There is some truth in what you say; still I think that you set a little too much value on money, and that it is in itself something so base that he who respects himself should never make a display of his love for it.

MUS. MAS. Yet you receive readily enough the money our man gives you.

DAN. MAS. Certainly; but my whole happiness does not depend upon it; and I can still wish that with all his wealth he had good taste.

MUS. MAS. I wish it as much as you do; and we are both working as hard as we can towards that end. But at the same time he gives us the opportunity of making ourselves known. He shall pay for others, and others shall praise for him.

DAN. MAS. Here he comes.

SCENE II.—MR. JOURDAIN (*in a dressing-gown and night-cap*), THE MUSIC MASTER, THE DANCING MASTER, THE PUPIL OF THE MUSIC MASTER, A LADY SINGER, TWO MEN SINGERS, DANCERS, TWO SERVANTS.

MR. JOUR. Well, gentlemen! and what have you got there? Are you ready to show me your little drollery?

DAN. MAS. How? What little drollery?

The Shopkeeper Turned Gentleman

MR. JOUR. Why, the ... what do you call it? Your prologue or dialogue of songs and dancing.

DAN. MAS. Ah, ah!

MUS. MAS. You see we are quite ready.

MR. JOUR. I have kept you waiting a little, but it is because I am to be dressed to-day like a man of rank, and my tailor sent me a pair of silk stockings which I thought I should never be able to get on.

MUS. MAS. We are here only to await your leisure.

MR. JOUR. I hope you will both stop till they have brought me my clothes, so that you may see me.

DAN. MAS. As you please.

MR. JOUR. You will see me equipped fashionably from head to foot.

MUS. MAS. We have no doubt of it.

MR. JOUR. I have had this dressing gown made for me.

DAN. MAS. It is very handsome,

MR. JOUR. My tailor told me that people of quality are dressed like this in the morning.

MUS. MAS. It becomes you wonderfully well.

MR. JOUR. Hullo! fellows! hullo! I say; my two lackeys, here!

1ST LACK. Do you want anything, Sir?

MR. JOUR. No; it was only to see if you heard me readily. (*To the* TWO MASTERS) What do you think of my liveries?

The Shopkeeper Turned Gentleman

DAN. MAS. They are magnificent.

MR. JOUR. (*opening his gown, and showing his tight breeches of scarlet velvet, and a green velvet morning jacket which he is wearing*). This is a kind of deshabille to go about early in the morning.

MUS. MAS. It is charming.

MR. JOUR. I say! lackey!

1ST LACK. Sir.

MR. JOUR. The other.

2ND LACK. Sir.

MR. JOUR. (*taking off his dressing-gown*). Hold my dressing-gown. (*To the* TWO MASTERS) Do you think I look well so?

DAN. MAS. Perfectly well; nothing could be better.

MR. JOUR. Now let us see a little of this affair of yours.

MUS. MAS. I should like, first of all, for you to hear an air which he (*pointing to his* PUPIL) has just composed for the serenade you asked of me. He is one of my pupils, who has an admirable talent for this kind of thing.

MR. JOUR. Yes; but you should not have had it done by a pupil; you were not too good for the business yourself.

MUS. MAS. You must not be deceived, Sir, by the name of pupil. These kind of pupils know sometimes as much as the greatest masters; and the air is as beautiful as possible. Only just listen to it.

MR. JOUR. (*to his* SERVANTS). Hand me my dressing-gown, so that may hear better.... Stay, I believe that I shall be better without.... No, give it me back again; that will be best.

THE PUPIL All night and day I languish on; the sick man none can save Since those bright eyes have laid him low, to your stern laws a slave; If thus to those you love a meed of care you bring, What pain, fair Iris, will you find your foemen's hearts to wring?

MR. JOUR. This song seems to me rather dismal; it sends one to sleep; could you not enliven it a bit here and there?

MUS. MAS. We must, Sir, suit the air to the words.

MR. JOUR. I was taught a very pretty one quite lately; stop a moment ... ahem ... What is it? How does it begin?

DAN. MAS. Upon my word, Sir, I do not know.

MR. JOUR. There is some lamb in it.

DAN. MAS. Lamb?

MR. JOUR. Yes, ah! I have it. (*He sings.*) /

When I had Jenny seen, I thought her kind as fair, I thought she'd gentler been Than lambkin on the green; But ah! but ah! she's far less mild, Far sterner, I declare, Than tigers are in forests wild.

Now, isn't it pretty?

MUS. MAS. The prettiest thing in the world.

DAN. MAS. And you sing it very well.

MR. JOUR. Do I? I have never learnt music.

The Shopkeeper Turned Gentleman

MUS. MAS. You ought to learn it, Sir, as you do dancing. These are two arts which are closely bound together.

DAN. MAS. And which open the human mind to the beauty of things.

MR. JOUR. Do people of rank learn music also?

MUS. MAS. Yes, Sir.

MR. JOUR. I will learn it, then; but I hardly know how I shall find time for it; for, besides the fencing master who teaches me, I have engaged a professor of philosophy, who is to begin this morning.

MUS. MAS. Philosophy is something, no doubt; but music, Sir, music....

DAN. MAS. Music and dancing, Sir; in music and dancing we have all that we need.

MUS. MAS. There is nothing so useful in a state as music.

DAN. MAS. There is nothing so necessary to men as dancing.

MUS. MAS. Without music no kingdom can exist.

DAN. MAS. Without dancing a man can do nothing.

MUS. MAS. All the disorders, all the wars that happen in the world, are caused by nothing but the want of music.

DAN. MAS. All the sorrows and troubles of mankind, all the fatal misfortunes which fill the pages of history, the blunders of statesmen, the failures of great captains, all these come from the want of a knowledge of dancing.

MR. JOUR. How is that?

MUS. MAS. Does not war arise from a want of concord between them?

The Shopkeeper Turned Gentleman

MR. JOUR. True.

MUS. MAS. And if all men learnt music, would not this be the means of keeping them in better harmony, and of seeing universal peace reign in the world?

MR. JOUR. You are quite right.

DAN. MAS. When a man has committed some fault, either in the management of his family affairs, or in the government of a state, or in the command of an army, do we not say, "So–and–so has made a false step in such an affair"?

MR. JOUR. Yes, we do say so.

DAN. MAS. And from whence can proceed the false step if it is not from ignorance of the art of dancing?

MR. JOUR. This is true, and you are both right.

DAN. MAS. This will give you an idea of the excellence and importance of dancing and music.

MR. JOUR. I understand it now.

MUS. MAS. Will you look at our two compositions?

MR. JOUR. Yes.

MUS. MAS. I have already told you that it is a short attempt which I made some time since to represent the different passions which can be expressed by music.

MR. JOUR. Very well.

MUS. MAS. (*to the* SINGERS). Come forward. (*To* MR. JOURDAIN) You must fancy that they are dressed like shepherds.

MR. JOUR. Why always shepherds? One sees nothing but that everywhere.

The Shopkeeper Turned Gentleman

DAN. **MAS**. When we make people speak to music, we must, for the sake of probability, adopt the pastoral. Singing has always been affected by shepherds, and it is not very likely that our princes or citizens would sing their passions in dialogue.

MR. JOUR. Well! well! Go on.

LADY SINGER. The realm of passion in a loving heart Full many a care may vex, full many a smart; In vain we fondly languish, softly sigh; We learn too late, whatever friends may cry, To value liberty before it fly.

1ST MAN SINGER. Sweeter than liberty are love's bright fires, Kindling in two fond hearts the same desires; Happiness could never live by love unfed, Pleasure itself would die if love were dead.

2ND MAN SINGER. Love would be sweet if love could constant be, But ah! sad fate, no faithful loves we see! The fair are false; no prayers their heart can move, And who will love when they inconstant prove?

1ST SING. Ah! love, how sweet thou art!

LADY SING. Ah! freedom is happier!

2ND SING. Thou inconstant heart!

1ST SING. To me how dear, how blest!

LADY SING. My soul enraptured see!

2ND SING. I shrink, I turn from thee!

1ST SING. Ah! leave this idle strife, and learn to love.

LADY SING. I will show thee one who'll constant prove.

2ND SING. Alas! where seek her?

LADY SING. To defend our name, I offer you my heart, nor heed your blame.

2ND SING. But, Lady, dare I trust that promise blest?

LADY SING. Experience will decide who loves the best.

2ND SING. Who fails in constancy or depth of love The gods from him their favour will remove.

ALL THREE. Such noble feelings should our souls inspire, And melt our heart beneath love's gentle fire. For love is sweet when hearts are true and pure, And love shall last while earth and heaven endure.

MR. JOUR. Is that all?

MUS. MAS. Yes.

MR. JOUR. I think it very well turned out, and there are in it some pretty enough little sayings.

DAN. MAS. You have here from me an essay of the most beautiful movements and most graceful attitudes with which a dance can be varied.

MR. JOUR. Are these shepherds also?

DAN. MAS. They are what you please. (*To the* DANCERS) Ho! ho! here!

Entry of the **BALLET**.

FOUR DANCERS *execute the various movements and steps which the* **DANCING MASTER** *orders them*.

ACT II.

The Shopkeeper Turned Gentleman

SCENE I.—MR. JOURDAIN, DANCING MASTER, MUSIC MASTER.

MR. JOUR. This performance is not bad, and these fellows don't do it badly.

MUS. MAS. When the dance is accompanied by the music, you will find it still more effective, and you will see something charming in the little ballet we have prepared for you.

MR. JOUR. It is for this afternoon, mind; and the person for whom I have ordered all this is to do me the honour of coming to dine here.

DAN. MAS. Everything is ready.

MUS. MAS. But, Sir, this is not enough; a gentleman magnificent in all his ideas like you, and who has taste for doing things handsomely, should have a concert at his house every Wednesday or Thursday.

MR. JOUR. But why should I? Do people of quality have concerts?

MUS. MAS. Yes, Sir.

MR. JOUR. Oh! very well! Then I too must have some. It'll be fine?

MUS. MAS. Very. You must have three voices: a treble, a counter-tenor, and a bass; which must be accompanied by a bass-viol, a theorbo lute, and a harpsichord for the thorough-basses, with two violins to play the harmonics.

MR. JOUR. You must also have a trumpet-marine. [Footnote: An instrument with one thick string.] The trumpet-marine is an instrument that I like, and a very harmonious one.

MUS. MAS. Leave all the arrangements to us.

MR. JOUR. Be sure you don't forget to send me, by and by, some singers to sing at table.

The Shopkeeper Turned Gentleman

MUS. MAS. You shall have all that is necessary.

MR. JOUR. But, above all, give us a nice ballet.

MUS. MAS. You will be pleased with it, and particularly with certain minuets which you shall see in it.

MR. JOUR. Ah! minuets are my favourite dance, and you should see me dance one. Come, my master.

DAN. MAS. A hat, Sir, if you please. (MR. JOURDAIN *takes the hat from his* SERVANT, *and puts it on over his night-cap; his master takes him by both hands, and makes him dance to a minuet air which he hums.*) La, la, la, la, la, la; la, la, la, la, la, la, la; la, la, la, la, la, la; la, la, la, la, la, la; la, la, la, la, la; in time, if you please; la, la, la, la, la; the right leg, la, la, la; do not shake your shoulders so much; la, la, la, la, la, la, la, la, la; your two arms are crippled; la, la, la, la, la; hold up your head; turn out your toes; la, la, la; your body erect.

MR. JOUR. Eh! eh!

MUS. MAS. Wonderfully well done.

MR. JOUR. Now I think of it! Teach me to make a bow to a marchioness. I shall have need of it presently.

DAN. MAS. A bow to a marchioness?

MR. JOUR. Yes; a marchioness, whose name is Dorimene.

DAN. MAS. Give me your hand.

MR. JOUR. No. You need only do it yourself. I shall be sure to remember.

DAN. MAS. If you want to salute her with great respect, you must first of all bow whilst stepping backward, then, advancing towards her, make three bows, and at the last bow bend down to her very knees.

MR. JOUR. Do it a little for me to see. (*After the* DANCING MASTER *has made three bows*) Good.

SCENE II.—MR. JOURDAIN, MUSIC MASTER, DANCING MASTER, A SERVANT.

SER. Sir, your fencing master is here.

MR. JOUR. Make him come in here for my lesson. (*To the* MUSIC *and* DANCING MASTERS) I wish you to see me perform.

SCENE III.—MR. JOURDAIN, FENCING MASTER, MUSIC MASTER, DANCING MASTER, A SERVANT *holding two foils*.

FEN. **MAS**. (*taking the two foils from the hands of the* SERVANT, *and giving one to* MR. JOURDAIN). Now, Sir, the salute. The body upright, resting slightly on the left thigh. The legs not so far apart; the feet in a line. The wrist in a line with the thigh. The point of the foil opposite the shoulder. The arm not quite so much extended. The left hand as high as the eye. The left shoulder more squared. The head erect; the look firm. Advance; the body steady. Engage my blade in quart, and retain the engagement. One, two. As you were. Once more, with the foot firm. One, two; a step to the rear. When you make an attack, Sir, the sword should move first, and the body be well held back. One, two. Engage my blade in tierce, and retain the engagement. Advance; the body steady. Advance; one, two. Recover. Once more. One, two. A step to the rear. On guard, Sir; on guard. (*The* FENCING MASTER *delivers two or three attacks, calling out*, "On guard!")

MR. JOUR. Ah!

MUS. **MAS**. You are doing wonders.

FEN. **MAS**. As I have already told you, the whole art of fencing consists of one of two things—in giving and not receiving; and as I showed you the other day by demonstrative reason, it is impossible for you to receive if you know how to turn aside your adversary's weapon from the line of your body; and this again depends only on a slight movement of the wrist to the inside or the out. [Footnote: Kindly corrected by Mr. Maclaren, The Gymnasium, Oxford.]

MR. JOUR. So that a man, without having any courage, is sure of killing his man, and of not being killed himself.

FEN. MAS. Exactly. Did you not see plainly the demonstration of it?

MR. JOUR. Yes.

FEN. MAS. And this shows you of what importance we must be in a state; and how much the science of arms is superior to all the other useless sciences, such as dancing, music....

DAN. MAS. Gently, Mr. Fencing Master; speak of dancing with respect, if you please.

MUS. MAS. Pray learn to treat more properly the excellence of music.

FEN. MAS. You certainly are odd sort of people to try and compare your sciences to mine.

MUS. MAS. Just see the man of importance!

DAN. MAS. A fine animal, to be sure, with his plastron.

FEN. MAS. Take care, my little dancing master, or I shall make you dance in fine style. And you, my little musician, I'll teach you to sing out.

DAN. MAS. And you, my beater of iron, I'll teach you your trade.

MR. JOUR. (*to the* DANCING MASTER). Are you mad to go and quarrel with a man, who understands tierce and quart, and knows how to kill another by demonstrative reason?

The Shopkeeper Turned Gentleman

DAN. MAS. I don't care a straw for his demonstrative reason, and his tierce and his quart.

MR. JOUR. (*to the* DANCING MASTER). Gently, I tell you.

FEN. MAS. (*to the* DANCING MASTER). How! You little impudent fellow!

MR. JOUR. Ah! my fencing master!

DAN. MAS. (*to the* FENCING MASTER). How! you great cart–horse!

MR. JOUR. Stop! my dancing master!

FEN. MAS. If I once begin with you....

MR. JOUR. (*to the* FENCING MASTER). Gently.

DAN. MAR. If I lay my hand upon you....

MR. JOUR. Softly.

FEN. MAS. I will beat you after such a fashion....

MR. JOUR. (*to the* FENCING MASTER). For goodness sake!

DAN. MAS. I'll thrash you in such a style....

MR. JOUR. (*to the* DANCING MASTER). I beg of you....

MUS. MAS. Let us teach him a little how to behave himself.

MR. JOUR. (*to the* MUSIC MASTER). Gracious heavens! Do stop.

SCENE IV.—PROFESSOR OF PHILOSOPHY, MR. JOURDAIN, MUSIC MASTER, DANCING MASTER, FENCING MASTER, A SERVANT.

MR. JOUR. Oh! you are in the very nick of time with your philosophy. Pray come here and restore peace among these people.

PROF. PHIL. What is going on? What is the matter, gentlemen?

MR. JOUR. They have got themselves into such a rage about the importance that ought to be attached to their different professions that they have almost come to blows over it.

PROF. PHIL. For shame, gentlemen; how can you thus forget yourselves? Have you not read the learned treatise which Seneca composed on anger? Is there anything more base and more shameful than the passion which changes a man into a savage beast, and ought not reason to govern all our actions?

DAN. MAS. How, Sir! He comes and insults us both in our professions; he despises dancing, which I teach, and music, which is his occupation.

PROF. PHIL. A wise man is above all the insults that can be offered him; and the best and noblest answer one can make to all kinds of provocation is moderation and patience.

FEN. MAS. They have both the impertinence to compare their professions to mine!

PROF. PHIL. Why should this offend you? It is not for vain glory and rank that men should strive among themselves. What distinguishes one man from another is wisdom and virtue.

DAN. MAS. I maintain that dancing is a science which we cannot honour too much. [Footnote: In fact, dancing was much more honoured in Moliere's time than it is now.]

MUS. MAS. And I that music is a science which all ages have revered.

The Shopkeeper Turned Gentleman

FEN. **MAS**. And I, I maintain against them both that the science of attack and defence is the best and most necessary of all sciences.

PROF. **PHIL**. And for what, then, do you count philosophy? I think you are all three very bold fellows to dare to speak before me with this arrogance, and impudently to give the name of science to things which are not even to be honoured with the name of art, but which can only be classed with the trades of prize-fighter, street-singer, and mountebank.

FEN. **MAS**. Get out, you dog of a philosopher.

MUS. **MAS**. Get along with you, you beggarly pedant.

DAN. **MAS**. Begone, you empty-headed college scout.

PROF. **PHIL**. How, scoundrels that you are!

(*The* PHILOSOPHER *rushes upon them, and they all three belabour him.*)

MR. **JOUR**. Mr. Philosopher.

PROF. **PHIL**. Infamous villains!

MR. **JOUR**. Mr. Philosopher!

FEN. **MAS**. Plague take the animal!

MR. **JOUR**. Gentlemen!

PROF. **PHIL**. Impudent cads!

MR. **JOUR**. Mr. Philosopher!

DAN. **MAS**. Deuce take the saddled ass!

MR. **JOUR**. Gentlemen!

PROF. PHIL. Scoundrels!

MR. JOUR. Mr. Philosopher!

MUS. MAS. Devil take the insolent fellow!

MR. JOUR. Gentlemen!

PROF. PHIL. Knaves, beggars, wretches, impostors!

MR. JOUR. Mr. Philosopher! Gentlemen! Mr. Philosopher! Gentlemen! Mr. Philosopher!

SCENE V.—MR. JOURDAIN, A SERVANT.

MR. JOUR. Well! fight as much as you like, I can't help it; but don't expect me to go and spoil my dressing-gown to separate you. I should be a fool indeed to thrust myself among them, and receive some blow or other that might hurt me.

SCENE VI.—PROFESSOR OF PHILOSOPHY, MR. JOURDAIN, A SERVANT.

PROF. PHIL. (*setting his collar in order*). Now for our lesson.

MR. JOUR. Ah! Sir, how sorry I am for the blows they have given you.

PROF. PHIL. It is of no consequence. A philosopher knows how to receive things calmly, and I shall compose against them a satire, in the style of Juvenal, which will cut them up in proper fashion. Let us drop this subject. What do you wish to learn?

MR. JOUR. Everything I can, for I have the greatest desire in the world to be learned; and it vexes me more than I can tell that my father and mother did not make me learn thoroughly all the sciences when I was young.

The Shopkeeper Turned Gentleman

PROF. PHIL. This is a praiseworthy feeling. *Nam sine doctrina vita est quasi mortis imago.* You understand this, and you have no doubt a knowledge of Latin?

MR. JOUR. Yes; but act as if I had none. Explain to me the meaning of it.

PROF. PHIL. The meaning of it is, that, *without science, life is an image of death.*

MR. JOUR. That Latin is quite right.

PROF. PHIL. Have you any principles, any rudiments of science?

MR. JOUR. Oh yes; I can read and write.

PROF. PHIL. With what would you like to begin? Shall I teach you logic?

MR. JOUR. And what may this logic be?

PROF. PHIL. It is that which teaches us the three operations of the mind.

MR. JOUR. What are they, these three operations of the mind?

PROF. PHIL. The first, the second, and the third. The first is to conceive well by means of universals; the second, to judge well by means of categories; and the third, to draw a conclusion aright by means of the figures *Barbara, Celarent, Darii, Ferio, Baralipton*,

MR. JOUR. Pooh! what repulsive words. This logic does not by any means suit me. Teach me something more enlivening.

PROF. PHIL. Will you learn moral philosophy?

MR. JOUR. Moral philosophy?

PROF. PHIL. Yes.

MR. JOUR. What does it say, this moral philosophy?

The Shopkeeper Turned Gentleman

PROF. PHIL. It treats of happiness, teaches men to moderate their passions, and....

MR. JOUR. No, none of that. I am devilishly hot-tempered, and, morality or no morality, I like to give full vent to my anger whenever I have a mind to it.

PROF. PHIL. Would you like to learn physics?

MR. JOUR. And what have physics to say for themselves?

PROF. PHIL. Physics are that science which explains the principles of natural things and the properties of bodies, which discourses of the nature of the elements, of metals, minerals, stones, plants, and animals; which teaches us the cause of all the meteors, the rainbow, the *ignis fatuus*, comets, lightning, thunder, thunderbolts, rain, snow, hail, wind, and whirlwinds.

MR. JOUR. There is too much hullaballoo in all that; too much riot and rumpus.

PROF. PHIL. What would you have me teach you then?

MR. JOUR. Teach me spelling.

PROF. PHIL. Very good.

MR. JOUR. Afterwards you will teach me the almanac, so that I may know when there is a moon, and when there isn't one.

PROF. PHIL. Be it so. In order to give a right interpretation to your thought, and to treat this matter philosophically, we must begin, according to the order of things, with an exact knowledge of the nature of the letters, and the different way in which each is pronounced. And on this head I have to tell you that letters are divided into vowels, so called because they express the voice, and into consonants, so called because they are sounded with the vowels, and only mark the different articulations of the voice. There are five vowels or voices, *a, e, i, o, u*. [Footnote: It is scarcely necessary to say that this description, such as it is, only applies to the French vowels as they are pronounced in *pate, the, ici, cote, du* respectively.]

The Shopkeeper Turned Gentleman

MR. JOUR. I understand all that.

PROF. PHIL. The vowel *a* is formed by opening the mouth very wide; *a*.

MR. JOUR. A, *a*; yes.

PROF. PHIL. The vowel *e* is formed by drawing the lower jaw a little nearer to the upper; *a, e*.

MR. JOUR. A, *e*; a, *e*; to be sure. Ah! how beautiful that is!

PROF. PHIL. And the vowel *i* by bringing the jaws still closer to one another, and stretching the two corners of the mouth towards the ears; *a, e, i*.

MR. JOUR. A, e, *i, i, i, i*. Quite true. Long live science!

PROF. PHIL. The vowel *o* is formed by opening the jaws, and drawing in the lips at the two corners, the upper and the lower; *o*.

MR. JOUR. O, *o*. Nothing can be more correct; *a, e, i, o, i, o*. It is admirable! *I, o, i, o*.

PROF. PHIL. The opening of the mouth exactly makes a little circle, which resembles an *o*.

MR. JOUR. O, *o, o*. You are right. *O*! Ah! what a fine thing it is to know something!

PROF. PHIL. The vowel *u* is formed by bringing the teeth near each other without entirely joining them, and thrusting out both the lips whilst also bringing them near together without quite joining them; *u*.

MR. JOUR. U, *u*. There is nothing more true; *u*.

PROF. PHIL. Your two lips lengthen as if you were pouting; so that, if you wish to make a grimace at anybody, and to laugh at him, you have only to *u* him.

The Shopkeeper Turned Gentleman

MR. JOUR. *U, u.* It's true. Oh! that I had studied when I was younger, so as to know all this.

PROF. PHIL. To-morrow we will speak of the other letters, which are the consonants.

MR. JOUR. Is there anything as curious in them as in these?

PROF. PHIL. Certainly. For instance, the consonant *d* is pronounced by striking the tip of the tongue above the upper teeth; *da*.

MR. JOUR. *Da, da.* [Footnote: Untranslatable. *Dada* equals "cock-horse" in nursery language] Yes. Ah! what beautiful things, what beautiful things!

PROF. PHIL. The *f*, by pressing the upper teeth upon the lower lip; *fa*.

MR. JOUR. *Fa, fa.* 'Tis the truth. Ah! my father and my mother, how angry I feel with you!

PROF. PHIL. And the *r*, by carrying the tip of the tongue up to the roof of the palate, so that, being grazed by the air which comes out with force, it yields to it, and, returning to the same place, causes a sort of tremour; *r, ra*.

MR. JOUR. *R-r-ra; r-r-r-r-r-ra.* That's true. Ah! what a clever man you are, and what time I have lost. *R-r-ra.*

PROF. PHIL. I will thoroughly explain all these curiosities to you.

MR. JOUR. Pray do. And now I want to entrust you with a great secret. I am in love with a lady of quality, and I should be glad if you would help me to write something to her in a short letter which I mean to drop at her feet.

PROF. PHIL. Very well.

MR. JOUR. That will be gallant; will it not?

PROF. PHIL. Undoubtedly. Is it verse you wish to write to her?

The Shopkeeper Turned Gentleman

MR. JOUR. Oh no; not verse.

PROF. PHIL. You only wish for prose?

MR. JOUR. No. I wish for neither verse nor prose.

PROF. PHIL. It must be one or the other.

MR. JOUR. Why?

PROF. PHIL. Because, Sir, there is nothing by which we can express ourselves except prose or verse.

MR. JOUR. There is nothing but prose or verse?

PROF. PHIL. No, Sir. Whatever is not prose is verse; and whatever is not verse is prose.

MR. JOUR. And when we speak, what is that, then?

PROF. PHIL. Prose.

MR. JOUR. What! When I say, "Nicole, bring me my slippers, and give me my night-cap," is that prose?

PROF. PHIL. Yes, Sir.

MR. JOUR. Upon my word, I have been speaking prose these forty years without being aware of it; and I am under the greatest obligation to you for informing me of it. Well, then, I wish to write to her in a letter, *Fair Marchioness, your beautiful eyes make me die of love*; but I would have this worded in a genteel manner, and turned prettily.

PROF. PHIL. Say that the fire of her eyes has reduced your heart to ashes; that you suffer day and night for her tortures....

MR. JOUR. No, no, no; I don't want any of that. I simply wish for what I tell you. *Fair Marchioness, your beautiful eyes make me die of love.*

PROF. PHIL. Still, you might amplify the thing a little?

MR. JOUR. No, I tell you, I will have nothing but those very words in the letter; but they must be put in a fashionable way, and arranged as they should be. Pray show me a little, so that I may see the different ways in which they can be put.

PROF. PHIL. They may be put, first of all, as you have said, *Fair Marchioness, your beautiful eyes make me die of love*; or else, *Of love die make me, fair Marchioness, your beautiful eyes*; or, *Your beautiful eyes of love make me, fair Marchioness, die*; or, *Die of love your beautiful eyes, fair Marchioness, make me*; or else, *Me make your beautiful eyes die, fair Marchioness, of love*.

MR. JOUR. But of all these ways, which is the best?

PROF. PHIL. The one you said: *Fair Marchioness, your beautiful eyes make me die of love*.

MR. JOUR. Yet I have never studied, and I did all that right off at the first shot. I thank you with all my heart, and I beg of you to come to-morrow morning early.

PROF. PHIL. I shall not fail.

SCENE VII.—MR. JOURDAIN, A SERVANT.

MR. JOUR. What? Has my suit of clothes not come yet?

SER. No, Sir.

MR. JOUR. That confounded tailor makes me wait a long time on a day like this, when I have so much business to attend to. I am furious. May the deuce fly away with the tailor! May the plague choke the tailor! May the ague shake that brute of a tailor! If I had him here now, that rascally tailor, that wretch of a tailor, I....

SCENE VIII.—MR. JOURDAIN, THE MASTER TAILOR, AN ASSISTANT TAILOR (*bringing a suit of clothes for* MR. JOURDAIN), A SERVANT.

MR. JOUR. Ha! here you are. I was just on the point of getting angry with you.

TAIL. I could not come sooner, although I set twenty people to work at your coat.

MR. JOUR. You have sent me such a small pair of silk stockings that I had no end of trouble to put them on, and two of the stitches are broken already.

TAIL. They are pretty sure to become only too large.

MR. JOUR. No doubt, if I keep on breaking the stitches. You also sent me a pair of shoes that hurt me horribly.

TAIL. Not at all, Sir.

MR. JOUR. How! not at all?

TAIL. No; they do not hurt you at all.

MR. JOUR. I tell you they do hurt me.

TAIL. You fancy so.

MR. JOUR. I fancy so because I feel it to be so. Did any one ever hear such an argument!

TAIL. See, we have the most beautiful and the best matched suit in the whole court. It is a work of art to have discovered a sober suit of clothes not black; and I bet that the most skilful tailors would not do as much after half a dozen trials.

MR. JOUR. Why, what does this mean? You have put all the flowers upside down.

The Shopkeeper Turned Gentleman

TAIL. You did not tell me you wished to have them the other way up.

MR. JOUR. Was it necessary to say that?

TAIL. Yes, certainly; for all the people of quality wear them in this way.

MR. JOUR. All people of quality wear the flowers bottom upwards?

TAIL. Yes, Sir.

MR. JOUR. Oh, then it's all right.

TAIL. If you wish it, I will put them the other way up.

MR. JOUR. No, no.

TAIL. You have only to say so.

MR. JOUR. No, no. I tell you that you have done right. Do you think my clothes fit me well?

TAIL. No doubt about it. I defy any painter with his pencil to draw you anything to fit more exactly. I have in my house a workman who to get up a rhinegrave is the greatest genius of our time, and another who in putting together a doublet is the hero of our age.

MR. JOUR. Are the wig and feathers as they should be?

TAIL. Everything is right.

MR. JOUR. (*looking carefully at the tailor's coat*). Oh! oh! Mr. Tailor, you have there some of the stuff of the last coat you made for me! I know it well.

TAIL. I thought the stuff so beautiful that I could not help cutting a coat from it for myself.

MR. JOUR. Yes; but you should not have cut it from mine.

TAIL. Will you put on your coat?

MR. JOUR. Yes; give it me.

TAIL. Wait a moment. Things are not done in that manner. I have brought my people with me to dress you to music; such coats as these are only put on with ceremony. Hullo there! Come in.

SCENE IX.—MR. JOURDAIN, MASTER TAILOR, ASSISTANT TAILORS (*dancing*), A SERVANT.

TAIL. Put this gentleman's suit on as you put on those of people of quality.

(*The four tailors, dancing, come near* MR. JOURDAIN; *two of them pull off the breeches he has had on for his exercises; two others take off his waistcoat; then, still dancing, they dress him in his new suit.* MR. JOURDAIN *walks round in the midst of them, and shows them his clothes for them to see whether they fit him.*)

TAILS. My noble gentleman, give something, if you please, to the tailors to drink your health with.

MR. JOUR. How do you call me?

TAILS. My noble gentleman.

MR. JOUR. See what it is to be dressed like a person of quality! Go about all your life dressed like a citizen, and nobody will ever call you a "noble gentleman." (*Giving some money.*) This is for "My noble gentleman."

TAILS. We are greatly obliged to you, my lord.

MR. JOUR. Oh! oh! Wait a minute, my friends. "My lord" deserves something; it is no small thing to be "My lord." Here is what his lordship gives you.

TAILS. My lord, we shall go and drink your grace's health.

MR. JOUR. "Your grace!" Oh! oh! oh! Stay, don't go yet. "Your grace" to me! (*Aside*) Upon my word, if he goes as far as highness, he will have the whole purse. (*Aloud*) Take this for "Your grace."

TAILS. My lord, we most humbly thank you for your liberality.

MR. JOUR. He did well to stop. I should have given him all.

Second entry of the **BALLET**.

The **FOUR ASSISTANTS** *rejoice, dancing, at the generosity of* **MR. JOURDAIN**.

ACT III.

SCENE I.—MR. JOURDAIN, TWO LACKEYS.

MR. JOUR. Follow me, that I may go and show my clothes about the town; and be very careful, both of you, to walk close to my heels, so that people may see that you belong to me.

LACK. Yes, Sir.

MR. JOUR. Just call Nicole. I have some orders to give her. You need not move; here she comes.

SCENE II.—MR. JOURDAIN, NICOLE, TWO LACKEYS.

MR. JOUR. Nicole!

NIC. What is it, Sir?

MR. JOUR. Listen.

NIC. (*laughing*). Hi, hi, hi, hi, hi.

The Shopkeeper Turned Gentleman

MR. JOUR. What are you laughing at?

NIC. Hi, hi, hi, hi, hi, hi.

MR. JOUR. What does the hussy mean?

NIC. Hi, hi, hi. What a figure you cut! Hi, hi, hi.

MR. JOUR. Eh? What?

NIC. Ah! ah! my goodness! Hi, hi, hi, hi, hi.

MR. JOUR. What an impertinent jade! Are you laughing at me?

NIC. Oh no, Sir. I should be very sorry to do so. Hi, hi, hi, hi, hi.

MR. JOUR. I'll slap your face if you laugh again.

NIC. I can't help it, Sir. Hi, hi, hi, hi, hi, hi.

MR. JOUR. Will you leave off?

NIC. Sir; I beg your pardon, Sir; but you are so very comical that I can't help laughing. Hi, hi, hi.

MR. JOUR. Did you ever see such impudence?

NIC. You are so odd like that. Hi, hi.

MR. JOUR. I'll....

NIC. I beg of you to excuse me. Hi, hi, hi, hi.

MR. JOUR. Look here, if you laugh again ever so little, I swear I will give you a box on the ears such as you never had before in all your life.

The Shopkeeper Turned Gentleman

NIC. Well, Sir, I have done. I won't laugh any more.

MR. JOUR. Mind you don't. You must for this afternoon clean....

NIC. Hi, hi.

MR. JOUR. You must clean thoroughly....

NIC. Hi, hi.

MR. JOUR. You must, I say, clean the drawing–room, and....

NIC. Hi, hi.

MR. JOUR. Again?

NIC. (*tumbling down with laughing*). There, Sir, beat me rather, but let me laugh to my heart's content. I am sure it will be better for me. Hi, hi, hi, hi, hi.

MR. JOUR. I am boiling with rage.

NIC. For pity's sake, Sir, let me laugh. Hi, hi, hi.

MR. JOUR. If I begin....

NIC. Si–r–r, I shall bur–r–st if I d–don't laugh. Hi, hi, hi.

MR. JOUR. But did you ever see such a hussy? She comes and laughs at me to my face, instead of attending to my orders.

NIC. What is it you wish me to do, Sir.

MR. JOUR. I want you to get this house ready for the company which is to come here by and by.

NIC. (*getting up*). Ah, well! All my wish to laugh is gone now; your company brings such disorder here that what you say is quite sufficient to put me out of temper.

MR. JOUR. I suppose that, to please you, I ought to shut my door against everybody?

NIC. Anyhow, you would do just as well to shut it against certain people, Sir.

SCENE III.—MRS. JOURDAIN, MR. JOURDAIN, NICOLE, TWO SERVANTS.

MRS. JOUR. Ah me! Here is some new vexation! Why, husband, what do you possibly mean by this strange get–up? Have you lost your senses that you go and deck yourself out like this, and do you wish to be the laughing–stock of everybody wherever you go?

MR. JOUR. Let me tell you, my good wife, that no one but a fool will laugh at me.

MRS. JOUR. No one has waited until to–day for that; and it is now some time since your ways of going on have been the amusement of everybody.

MR. JOUR. And who may everybody be, please?

MRS. JOUR. Everybody is a body who is in the right, and who has more sense than you. For my part, I am quite shocked at the life you lead. I don't know our home again. One would think, by what goes on, that it was one everlasting carnival here; and as soon as day breaks, for fear we should have any rest in it, we have a regular din of fiddles and singers, that are a positive nuisance to all the neighbourhood.

NIC. What mistress says is quite right. There is no longer any chance of having the house clean with all that heap of people you bring in. Their feet seem to have gone purposely to pick up the mud in the four quarters of the town in order to bring it in here afterwards; and poor Francoise is almost off her legs with the constant scrubbing of the floors, which your masters come and dirty every day as regular as clockwork.

MR. JOUR. I say there, our servant Nicole; you have a pretty sharp tongue of your own for a country wench.

The Shopkeeper Turned Gentleman

MRS. JOUR. Nicole is right, and she has more sense by far than you have. I should like to know, for instance, what you mean to do with a dancing master at your age?

NIC. And with that big fencing master, who comes here stamping enough to shake the whole house down and to tear up the floor tiles of our rooms.

MR. JOUR. Gently, my servant and my wife.

MRS. JOUR. Do you mean to learn dancing for the time when you can't stand on your legs any longer?

NIC. Do you intend to kill anybody?

MR. JOUR. Hold your tongues, I say. You are only ignorant women, both of you, and understand nothing concerning the prerogative of all this.

MRS. JOUR. You would do much better to think of seeing your daughter married, for she is now of an age to be provided for.

MR. JOUR. I shall think of seeing my daughter married when a suitable match presents itself; but, in the meantime, I wish to think of acquiring fine learning.

NIC. I have heard say also, mistress, that, to go the whole hog, he has now taken a professor of philosophy.

MR. JOUR. To be sure I have. I wish to be clever, and reason concerning things with people of quality.

MRS. JOUR. Had you not better go to school one of these days, and get the birch, at your age?

MR. JOUR. Why not? Would to heaven I were flogged this very instant, before all the world, so that I might know all they learn at school.

NIC. Yes, to be sure; that would much improve the shape of your leg.

The Shopkeeper Turned Gentleman

MR. JOUR. Of course.

MRS. JOUR. And all this is very necessary for the management of your house.

MR. JOUR. Certainly. You both speak like asses; and I am ashamed of your ignorance. (*To* MRS. JOURDAIN) Let me see, for instance, if you know what you are speaking this very moment.

MRS. JOUR. Yes, I know that what I speak is rightly spoken; and that you should think of leading a different life.

MR. JOUR. I do not mean that. I ask you what the words are which you are now speaking.

MRS. JOUR. They are sensible words, I tell you, and that is more than your conduct is.

MR. JOUR. I am not speaking of that. I ask you what it is that I am now saying to you. That which I am now speaking to you, what is it?

MRS. JOUR. Rubbish.

MR. JOUR. No! no! I don't mean that. What we both speak; the language we are speaking this very moment.

MRS. JOUR. Well?

MR. JOUR. How is it called?

MRS. JOUR. It is called whatever you like to call it.

MR. JOUR. It is prose, you ignorant woman.

MRS. JOUR. Prose?

MR. JOUR. Whatever is prose is not verse, and whatever is not verse is prose. There! you see what it is to study. (*To* NICOLE) And you, do you even know what you must do to say *u*?

NIC. Eh? What?

MR. JOUR. Yes; what do you do when you say *u*?

NIC. What I do?

MR. JOUR. Say *u* a little to try.

NIC. Well, *u*.

MR. JOUR. What is it you do?

NIC. I say *u*.

MR. JOUR. Yes; but when you say *u*, what is it you do?

NIC. I do what you ask me to do.

MR. JOUR. Oh! What a strange thing it is to have to do with dunces! You pout your lips outwards, and bring your upper jaw near your lower jaw like this, *u*; I make a face; *u*. Do you see?

NIC. Yes, that's beautiful.

MRS. JOUR. It's admirable!

MR. JOUR. What would you say then if you had seen *o*, and *da, da*, and *fa, fa*?

MRS. JOUR. What is all this absurd stuff?

NIC. And what are we the better for all this?

MR. JOUR. I have no patience with such ignorant women.

The Shopkeeper Turned Gentleman

MRS. JOUR. Believe me, pack off all those people with their ridiculous fooleries.

NIC. And particularly that great scraggy fencing master, who fills the whole place with dust.

MR. JOUR. Goodness me! The fencing master seems to set your teeth on edge. Come here, and I will show you at once your senseless impertinence. (*He asks for two foils, and gives one to* NICOLE.) Here, reason demonstrative the line of the body. When you thrust in quart, you have only to do so; and, when you thrust in tierce, only to do so! That is the way never to be killed; and is it not a fine thing to be quite safe when one fights against anybody? There, thrust at me a little to try.

NIC. Well, what? (NICOLE *gives him several thrusts*)

MR. JOUR. Gently! Hold! Oh! Softly. Deuce take the wench!

NIC: You tell me to thrust at you.

MR. JOUR. Yes; but you thrust in tierce before thrusting at me in quart, and you haven't the patience to wait till I parry.

MRS: JOUR. You are crazy, husband, with all your fads; and this has come upon you since you have taken it into your head to frequent the gentlefolk.

MR. JOUR. By frequenting the gentlefolk I show my judgment. It is surely better than keeping company with your citizens.

MRS. JOUR. Yes: there is much good to be got by frequenting your nobility, and you have done a noble stroke of business with that fine count with whom you are so wrapped up.

MR. JOUR. Peace. Be careful what you say. Let me tell you, wife, that you do not know of whom you are speaking when you speak of him! He is a man of more importance than you can imagine, a nobleman who is held in great honour at court, and who speaks to the king just as I speak to you. Is it not a thing which does me great honour that such a person should be seen so often in my house, should call me his dear friend, and should treat me as if I were his equal? He has more kindness for me than you could ever guess, and he treats me before the world with such affection that I am perfectly ashamed.

MRS. JOUR. Yes; he is kind to you, and flatters you, but he borrows your money of you.

MR. JOUR. Well? Is it not a great honour to lend money to a man of his position? And could I do less for a lord who calls me his dear friend?

MRS. JOUR. And this lord, what does he do for you?

MR. JOUR. Things that would astound you if you only knew them.

MRS. JOUR. But what?

MR. JOUR. There! I can't explain myself. It is quite sufficient that, if I have lent him money, he will give it back to me, and that before long.

MRS. JOUR. Yes, trust him for that.

MR. JOUR. Certainly I will. Has he not said so?

MRS. JOUR. Yes, yes; and he won't fail not to do it.

MR. JOUR. He has given me his word as a gentleman.

MRS. JOUR. Mere stuff.

MR. JOUR. Dear me! You are very obstinate, wife! I tell you that he will keep his word; I am quite sure of it.

MRS. JOUR. And I am quite sure that he won't; and that all the caresses he loads you with are only meant to deceive you.

MR. JOUR. Be silent; here he comes.

MRS. JOUR. That's to finish up. He comes, no doubt, to borrow from you again; the very sight of him takes my appetite away.

MR: JOUR. Hold your tongue, I tell you.

SCENE IV.—DORANTE, MR. JOURDAIN, MRS. JOURDAIN, NICOLE.

DOR. Mr. Jourdain, my dear friend, how do you do?

MR. JOUR. Very well, Sir; at your service.

DOR. And Mrs. Jourdain, how does she do?

MRS. JOUR. Mrs. Jourdain does as well as may be.

DOR. I declare, Mr. Jourdain, that you have the most genteel dress in the world.

MR. JOUR. You see.

DOR. You look exceedingly well in this dress, and we have no young men at court better made than you.

MR. JOUR. He! he!

MRS. JOUR. (*aside*). He scratches him where it itches.

DOR. Turn round. This is quite gallant.

MRS. JOUR. (*aside*). Yes, as fine a fool behind as before.

DOR. Indeed, Mr. Jourdain, I was very impatient to see you. You are the man I esteem most in the world, and I was talking of you again this very morning at the king's levee.

The Shopkeeper Turned Gentleman

MR. JOUR. You do me too much honour, Sir. (*To* MRS. JOURDAIN) At the king's levee.

DOR. Come, put on your hat.

MR. JOUR. Sir, I know the respect I owe you;

DOR. Pray, put on your hat. No ceremony between us, I beg.

MR. JOUR. Sir!

DOR. Nay! nay! Put on your hat, I tell you, Mr. Jourdain; you are my friend.

MR. JOUR. Sir, I am your humble servant.

DOR. I will not put mine on unless you do.

MR. JOUR. (*putting on his hat*). I had rather be unmannerly than troublesome.

DOR. I am your debtor, as you know.

MRS. JOUR. (*aside*). Yes, we know it but too well.

DOR. On several occasions you have generously lent me some money, and you have obliged me, I must acknowledge, with the best grace in the world.

MR. JOUR. Sir, I beg of you.

DOR. But I know how to pay back what is lent to me, and how to acknowledge services rendered.

MR. JOUR. I have no doubt about it, Sir.

DOR. I want to acquit myself towards you, and I have come to settle my accounts.

The Shopkeeper Turned Gentleman

MR. JOUR. (*aside to* MRS. JOURDAIN). Well? Do you see how wrong you were, wife?

DOR. I like to get out of debt as soon as I can.

MR. JOUR. (*aside to* MRS. JOURDAIN). Did I not tell you so?

DOR. Let us see how much I owe you.

MR. JOUR. (*aside to* MRS. JOURDAIN). There you are, with your absurd suspicions.

DOR. Do you quite remember how much you have lent me?

MR. JOUR. I believe so. I have made a little memorandum of it. Here it is. At one time I gave you two hundred louis.

DOR. Quite true.

MR. JOUR. At another time, one hundred and twenty.

DOR. Yes.

MR. JOUR. At another time, one hundred and forty.

DOR. You are quite right.

MR. JOUR. These three payments make four hundred and sixty louis, which comes to five thousand and sixty livres.

DOR. This account is quite correct; five thousand and sixty livres.

MR. JOUR. One thousand eight hundred and thirty–two livres to your plume seller.

DOR. Just so.

MR. JOUR. Two thousand seven hundred and eighty livres to your tailor.

The Shopkeeper Turned Gentleman

DOR. It is true.

MR. JOUR. Four thousand three hundred and seventy-nine livres, twelve sous, eight deniers, to your tradesman.

DOR. Twelve sous, eight deniers; the account is perfectly right.

MR. JOUR. And one thousand seven hundred and forty-eight livres, seven sous, four deniers, to your saddler.

DOR. It is so. How much does all this come to?

MR. JOUR. Sum-total, fifteen thousand eight hundred livres.

DOR. The sum-total is exact; fifteen thousand eight hundred livres. Add to this two hundred pistoles which you are going to lend me, and it will make exactly eighteen thousand francs, which I will pay you at the first opportunity.

MRS. JOUR. (*aside to* MR. JOURDAIN). Well? Did I not guess right?

MR. JOUR. (*aside to* MRS. JOURDAIN). Peace!

DOR. Will it be inconvenient to you to lend me what I say?

MR. JOUR. Oh dear! no.

MRS. JOUR. (*aside to* MR. JOURDAIN). That man makes a milch-cow of you.

MR. JOUR. (*aside to* MRS. JOURDAIN). Be silent!

DOR. If I at all inconvenience you, I will get it elsewhere.

MR. JOUR. No, Sir.

MRS. JOUR. (*aside to* MR. JOURDAIN). He won't be satisfied until he has ruined you.

MR. JOUR. (*aside to* MRS. JOURDAIN). Hold your tongue, I say.

DOR. You have only to tell me if this will embarrass you.

MR. JOUR. Not at all, Sir.

MRS. JOUR. (*aside to* MR. JOURDAIN). He is a regular deceiver.

MR. JOUR. (*aside to* MRS. JOURDAIN). Do hold your peace.

MRS. JOUR. (*aside to* MR. JOURDAIN). He will drain you to the last penny.

MR. JOUR. (*aside to* MRS. JOURDAIN). Will you hold your tongue?

DOR. There are a great many people who would advance me money with pleasure; but as I look upon you as my best friend, I was afraid of wronging you if I asked it of anyone else.

MR. JOUR. You do me too much honour, Sir. I will go and fetch what you want.

MRS. JOUR. (*aside to* MR. JOURDAIN). What! are you going to give him that also?

MR. JOUR. (*aside* to MRS. JOURDAIN). What can I do? How can I refuse a man of such rank, a man who spoke of me this morning at the king's levee.

MRS. JOUR. (*aside* to MR. JOURDAIN). There, go; you are nothing but a dupe.

SCENE V.—DORANTE, MRS. JOURDAIN, NICOLE.

DOR. You appear to me quite low-spirited! What can be the matter with you, Mrs. Jourdain?

MRS. JOUR. My head is bigger than my fist, and yet it isn't swollen.

DOR. Where is your daughter, that I have not seen her?

MRS. JOUR. My daughter is very well where she is.

DOR. How does she get on?

MRS. JOUR. She gets on on her two legs.

DOR. Would you not like one of these days to come with her to see the ballet and the play which are being acted at court?

MRS. JOUR. Ah! yes. We have a great fancy for laughing, a great fancy have we!

DOR. I think, Mrs. Jourdain, that you must have had plenty of lovers in your young days, so handsome, and so sweet-tempered as you must have been.

MRS. JOUR. My goodness, Sir! Has Mrs. Jourdain grown decrepit, and does her head already shake on her shoulders?

DOR. Oh! Mrs Jourdain, I really beg your pardon! I had forgotten that you are young, and I am very often absent. I beg of you to excuse my impertinence.

SCENE VI.—MR. JOURDAIN, MRS. JOURDAIN, DORANTE, NICOLE.

MR. JOUR. (*to* DORANTE). Here are two hundred louis in full.

DOR. I assure you, Mr. Jourdain, that you may dispose of me in any way you like, and that I long to render you some service at court.

MR. JOUR. I am much obliged to you.

DOR. If Mrs. Jourdain wishes to see the royal entertainment, [Footnote: 'The Magnificent Lovers.'] I will obtain the best places in the room for her.

MRS. JOUR. Mrs. Jourdain is your humble servant.

The Shopkeeper Turned Gentleman

DOR. (*aside to* MR. JOURDAIN). Our lovely marchioness, as I told you in my note, is coming here this afternoon for the ballet and the banquet, as I have at last prevailed on her to accept the entertainment you wish to give her. [Footnote: *Cadeau* does not mean "present," as at first sight it seems to mean. Compare also the next speech of Dorante.]

MR. JOUR. Let us go a little further. I need not tell you the reason.

DOR. It is a whole week since I saw you; and I did not send you any news of the diamond which you placed in my hands to make her a present of from you; it is because I found it the most difficult thing in the world to make her accept it; and it is only to-day that she could conquer her scruples about it.

MR. JOUR. How does she like it?

DOR. Exceedingly; and, unless I am greatly mistaken, the beauty of that diamond will produce an admirable effect on her mind towards you.

MR. JOUR. Ah, may it be so!

MRS. JOUR. (*to* NICOLE). When once he is with him, he can't leave him.

DOR. I described to her in glowing colours the expense of such a present, and the greatness of your love.

MR. JOUR. Your kindness is too much for me, Sir, and I feel perfectly ashamed to see a man of such high standing condescend to do for me the things you do.

DOR. Nonsense! Do friends stand upon such scruples? and would you not do for me the very same thing if the opportunity presented itself?

MR. JOUR. Oh, decidedly, and with all my heart!

MRS. JOUR. (*aside to* NICOLE). How hard for me to bear with his presence.

DOR. For my part, I hesitate at nothing when I want to serve a friend; and as soon as you told me of your admiration for this charming marchioness, with whom I was acquainted, you saw me at once put myself at your disposal to serve your love.

MR. JOUR. It is perfectly true. Such kindness confounds me.

MRS. JOUR. (*to* NICOLE). Will he never go?

NIC. (*to* MRS. JOURDAIN). They are very thick together.

DOR. You went the right way to work to touch her heart. There is nothing women like more than the expenses one makes for them; and your frequent serenades, your numerous bouquets, the magnificent display of fireworks which she saw on the water, the diamond which she received from you, and the entertainment you are preparing for her, all this tells more in favour of your love than all the speeches you could make to her about it.

MR. JOUR. There is no expense I would not make to find access to her heart. A woman of quality has for me the most dazzling charms, and it is an honour which I would purchase at any price.

MRS. JOUR. (*aside to* NICOLE). What on earth can they have to say together? Go and listen!

DOR. You will enjoy to-day the pleasure of seeing her; and your eyes will have full leisure to satisfy themselves.

MR. JOUR. In order to be free, I have arranged for my wife to go and dine with my sister, and she will spend the whole-afternoon there.

DOR. You have acted wisely, for your wife might be in the way. I have given the necessary orders to the cook, and for everything which may be necessary for the ballet. It is my own invention, and if the execution comes up to the conception, I am sure that it will be found....

MR. JOUR. (*seeing* NICOLE *listening, and giving her a box on the ears*). Ha! you rude, impertinent hussy! (*To* DORANTE) Let us go out, if you please.

SCENE VII.—MRS. JOURDAIN, NICOLE.

NIC. Well, Madam, my curiosity has cost me something; but all the same I believe that there is something in the wind, for they were speaking of an affair where they do not wish you to be present.

MRS. JOUR. This is not the first time, Nicole, that I have had some suspicions about my husband. Either I am greatly mistaken or there is some love affair on foot; and I am doing my best to discover what it maybe. But, first of all, let us think of my daughter. You know that Cleonte loves her; he is a man after my own heart, and I wish to help him, and give him to Lucile if I can.

NIC. To tell you the truth, Madam, I am delighted to find you think so; for if the master pleases you, the servant pleases me as well, and I wish our own marriage could take place at the same time as theirs.

MRS. JOUR. Go, then, and speak to him about what I told you; and tell him to come presently, that we may both together ask my husband to grant him my daughter.

NIC. I run with joy, Madam, and I could not receive a more pleasant order. (*Alone*.) How happy I am going to make certain people!

SCENE VIII.—NICOLE, CLEONTE, COVIELLE.

NIC. Ah, what a lucky meeting! I am a messenger of joy, and I came....

CLE. Leave me, false woman, and don't think of deceiving me with your treacherous words.

NIC. Do you receive me in that way?

CLE. Leave me, I say, and go and tell your faithless mistress that she never shall again deceive the too credulous Cleonte.

NIC. What a change? My poor Covielle, tell me, I pray, what all this means.

COV. Your poor Covielle, indeed, you wicked girl! Go, minx! decamp; get out of my sight as fast as you can, and leave me alone!

NIC. What! and do you also...?

COV. Get out of my sight, I say; I will never speak to you any more, as long as I live.

NIC. (*aside*). Mercy on us! What has happened to both of them? I must go and tell my mistress this pretty piece of news.

SCENE IX.—CLEONTE, COVIELLE.

CLE. What! to treat a lover in that fashion, and the most faithful and affectionate of all lovers!

COV. It is shameful what they have done to both of us!

CLE. I show her all possible ardour and tenderness; I love nothing in the world better, and have nothing in my thoughts but her; she is all my care, all my desire, all my joy; I speak of nothing but her, think of nothing but her, dream of nothing but her. I live but for her; my heart beats but for her; and, behold the reward of so much devotion! I am two whole days without seeing her, two days which seem to me centuries of frightful length; I meet her by accident, my heart at the sight of her feels transported; joy sparkles in my face. I fly to her with delight, and the faithless one turns away her eyes, and passes by me hastily, as if she had never seen me before in her life!

COV. I can only repeat the same story.

CLE. Can anything be compared, Covielle, to the perfidy of the ungrateful Lucile?

COV. And to that, Sir, of that hussy Nicole?

CLE. After so many passionate sacrifices, sighs, and vows which I have paid to her charms!

The Shopkeeper Turned Gentleman

COV. After so many attentions, cares, and services I have rendered her in the kitchen!

CLE. So many tears that I have shed at her feet!

COV. So many buckets of water that I have drawn for her from the well!

CLE. Such warmth as I have shown in loving her more than myself!

COV. Such heat as I have endured in turning the spit for her!

CLE. She avoids me with contempt!

COV. She rudely turns her back upon me!

CLE. This perfidy deserves the greatest chastisement.

COV. This treachery deserves a thousand blows.

CLE. Mind, you never speak to me of her any more.

COV. I, Sir? Heaven forbid!

CLE. Do not venture to palliate her wrongs before me.

COV. Never fear.

CLE. No; for all you would say in her defence would be lost upon me.

COV. Who dreams of such a thing?

CLE. I wish to nurse up my wrath against her, and to break off all intercourse with her.

COV. I am quite willing.

CLE. This count who goes to her house has turned her head, no doubt; and rank, I see, dazzles her mind. But I must, for my own honour, prevent her triumphing in her inconstancy. I will do as much as she does towards a change which I plainly see she desires, and I will not let her have all the pleasure of having dismissed me.

COV. You are in the right, and I enter into all your feelings.

CLE. Help me in my resentment, and support my resolution against the remainder of my love that might still plead for her. Tell me, I pray you, all the evil you can think of her. Draw a description of her person which may bring her down in my estimation, and, in order to make me dislike her more surely, show me all the defects you can see in her.

COV. She, indeed, Sir! a fine specimen, a fine piece of affectation to be in love with! I see nothing in her but the most common attractions, and you will find a thousand girls more worthy of your love than she is. To begin with, her eyes are small... [Footnote: It is Moliere's wife that is here described.]

CLE. Yes, it is true, her eyes are small, Covielle; but they are full of fire, the most sparkling, the most searching in the world, and the tenderest also that could be found.

COV. Her mouth is large....

CLE. Yes; but you find there charms that can be found in no other. The sight of that mouth inspires me with love; it is the most attractive and the most amorous mouth in the world!

COV. As to her height, she is not tall.

CLE. No; but she is well shaped and graceful.

COV. She affects great carelessness in her speech, and her movements....

CLE. It is true; but she is graceful in all she does, and her manners are attractive, and possess a certain charm which at once takes possession of one's heart.

COV. As for wit....

CLE. Ah, Covielle! her wit is of the most refined, the most delicate kind.

COV. Her conversation....

CLE. Her conversation is charming.

COV. It is always grave.

CLE. Would you prefer an unrestrained gaiety, a perpetual liveliness? and can you find anything more unpleasant than those women who giggle at everything?

COV. But, in short, she is as whimsical as any woman can be.

CLE. Yes, she is, I agree with you there; but everything becomes those we love. We bear everything from them.

COV. Since you go on so, I see pretty well that you are determined to love her still.

CLE. I? I had rather die this moment, and I mean in future to hate her as much as I loved her before.

COV. How can you if you think her so perfect?

CLE. In this way shall my revenge shine; in this way shall the strength of my decision to hate her be better displayed; if thinking her most beautiful, most charming, most amiable, I still part from her. Here she is.

SCENE X.—LUCILE, CLEONTE, COVIELLE, NICOLE.

NIC. (*to* LUCILE). I was quite shocked at it.

LUC. It can only be what I tell you, Nicole; but there he is.

CLE. (*to* COVIELLE). I will not condescend even to speak to her.

COV. I will do like you.

The Shopkeeper Turned Gentleman

LUC. What is it, Cleonte? What can be the matter with you?

NIC. What ails you, Covielle?

LUC. What trouble afflicts you?

NIC. What fit of bad temper has got hold of you?

LUC. Are you dumb, Cleonte?

NIC. Have you lost your tongue, Covielle?

CLE. How deceitful she is!

COV. How Judas–like!

LUC. I see that our meeting of this morning has troubled your mind.

CLE. (*to* COVIELLE). Ah! ah! we are conscious of what we have done?

NIC. Our reception of this morning has put you out.

COV. (*to* CLEONTE). We know where the shoe pinches.

LUC. Is it not true, Cleonte; is not this the cause of your vexation?

CLE. Yes, faithless girl, it is, since I am to speak; but I must inform you that you shall not have, as you fancy, all the glory of your faithlessness; I wish to be the first to break with you, and you shall not have the pleasure of driving me away. I shall find it hard, I know, to conquer the love I feel for you; it will bring grief to me; I am sure, to suffer for a while; but I will overcome it, and I had rather stab myself to the heart than be weak enough to return to you.

COV. (*to* NICOLE). As the master says, so says the man.

The Shopkeeper Turned Gentleman

LUC. This is much ado about nothing, Cleonte, and I wish to tell you what made me avoid you this morning.

CLE. (*trying to go away to avoid* LUCILE). I will hear nothing.

NIC. (*to* COVIELLE). I want to tell you why we passed you so quickly.

COV. (*trying also to go away to avoid* NICOLE). I will hear nothing.

LUC. (*following* CLEONTE). Know, then, that this morning....

CLE. (*still walking away without looking at* LUCILE). No, I tell you.

NIC. (*following* COVIELLE). Let me tell you....

COV. (*still walking away without looking at* NICOLE). No, you jilt!

LUC. Listen.

CLE. Don't trouble me.

NIC. Let me tell you.

COV. I am deaf.

LUC. Cleonte!

CLE. No.

NIC. Covielle!

COV. No.

LUC. Wait.

CLE. Nonsense.

The Shopkeeper Turned Gentleman

NIC. Listen to me.

COV. Rubbish.

LUC. One moment.

CLE. Not a bit.

NIC. A little patience.

COV. Fiddle–de–dee!

LUC. A couple of words.

CLE. No; all is over.

NIC. One word.

COV. Not one.

LUC. (*stopping*). Very well! Since you will not listen to me, keep your own thoughts to yourself, and do as you please.

NIC. (*stopping also*). Since you act in that fashion, think what you like.

CLE. (*turning towards* LUCILE). Well, what was the reason for such a welcome?

LUC. (*going away in her turn, to avoid* CLEONTE). I don't choose to tell you now.

COV. (*turning towards* NICOLE). Give us that story.

NIC. (*going away also, to avoid* COVIELLE). I don't wish to tell it you now.

CLE. (*following* LUCILE). Tell me....

LUC. (*walking away without looking at* CLEONTE). No; I will tell you nothing.

The Shopkeeper Turned Gentleman

COV. (*following* NICOLE). Relate to me....

NIC. (*walking away without looking at* COVIELLE). No; I shall relate nothing.

CLE. For mercy's sake!

LUC. No, I tell you.

COV. For pity's sake!

NIC. No; not another word.

CLE. I beseech you.

LUC. Leave me.

COV. I entreat you.

NIC. Get away from here.

CLE. Lucile!

LUC. No.

COV. Nicole!

NIC. Nothing.

CLE. For heaven's sake.

LUC. I will not.

COV. Speak to me.

NIC. I won't.

CLE. Clear up my doubts.

LUC. No; I will do nothing of the kind.

COV. Ease my mind.

NIC. No; it is not my wish to do so.

CLE. Very well! Since you care so little to relieve my grief, and to justify yourself of the unworthy treatment my love has received from you, you see me for the last time; and I am going away from you to die of grief and love.

COV. (*to* NICOLE). And I will follow his steps.

LUC. (*to* CLEONTE, *who is going*). Cleonte!

NIC. (*to* COVIELLE, *who is going*). Covielle!

CLE. (*stopping*). Hey?

COV. (*stopping also*). What do you say?

LUC. Where are you going?

CLE. Where I have told you.

COV. We are going to die.

LUC. You are going to die, Cleonte?

CLE. Yes, cruel one, since you wish it.

LUC. I! I wish you to die!

CLE. Yes, you wish it.

LUC. Who told you such a thing?

CLE. Is it not wishing it, to refuse to clear up my suspicions?

LUC. Is it my fault? If you had but listened to me, I would have told you at once that the treatment you complain of was caused by the presence of an old aunt, who persists in saying that the mere approach of a man is dishonour to a girl; she is always lecturing us about it, and depicts all men to us as so many scamps whom we ought always to avoid.

NIC. (*to* COVIELLE.) This is the whole secret of the affair.

CLE. (*to* LUCILE). Are you not deceiving me, Lucile?

COV. (*to* NICOLE). Are you not imposing upon me?

LUC. It is the exact truth.

NIC. That's how it is.

COV. (*to* CLEONTE). Shall we surrender after this?

CLE. Ah! Lucile! How you can with one word bring back peace to my heart; and how easily we suffer ourselves to be persuaded by those we love.

COV. How easily these queer animals succeed in getting round us.

SCENE XI.—MRS. JOURDAIN, CLEONTE, LUCILE, COVIELLE, NICOLE.

MRS. JOUR. I am very glad to see you, Cleonte. You are just in time, for my husband will be here in a moment. Seize that opportunity of asking him to give you Lucile in marriage.

CLE. Oh! how welcome these kind words are, and how well they correspond to the inmost wishes of my heart. Could I ever receive an order more flattering, a favour more precious?

SCENE XII.—CLEONTE, MR. JOURDAIN, MRS. JOURDAIN, LUCILE, COVIELLE, NICOLE.

CLE. Sir, I would not ask anybody to come instead of me to make you a request which I have long wished to make. The matter interests me too much for me not to do it myself. Allow me to tell you then, without further words, that the honour of becoming your son−in−law is a favour I earnestly solicit, and one which I beseech you to grant me.

MR. JOUR. Before I give you an answer, Sir, I beg you to tell me if you are a nobleman.

CLE. Sir, most people would answer that question without any hesitation whatever. The word is easily spoken; a title is generally adopted without scruple, and present custom seems to sanction the theft. For my part, however, I must confess that I look upon any kind of imposture as unworthy of an honest man. I think it base to hide what heaven has made us, to adorn ourselves before the world with a title, and to wish to pass for what we are not. I am the son of parents who have filled honourable offices. I have acquitted myself with honour in the army, where I served for six years, and I am rich enough to hold a tolerable position in the world; but for all this, I will not assume a name that others might think I could pretend to in my position, and I tell you openly that I cannot be reckoned a nobleman.

MR. JOUR. Shake hands, then, my daughter is no wife for you.

CLE. How! May I know...?

MR. JOUR. You are not a nobleman, therefore you shall not have my daughter.

MRS. JOUR. What is it you mean by your nobleman? Are we ourselves descended from St. Louis?

MR. JOUR. Be silent, wife; I see what you are driving at.

MRS. JOUR. Are we not both descended from good, simple tradesmen?

The Shopkeeper Turned Gentleman

MR. JOUR. Is not that a wicked slander?

MRS. JOUR. Was not your father a tradesman as well as mine?

MR. JOUR. Plague take the woman! She has never done with that. If your father was a tradesman, so much the worse for him; as for mine, it is only ill-informed people who say so, and all I have to tell you is that I will have a gentleman for my son-in-law.

MRS. JOUR. Your daughter must have a husband who suits her; and it is better for her to marry an honest man, rich and handsome, than a deformed and beggarly gentleman.

NIC. That's quite true. We have the son of the squire in our village, who is the most awkwardly built and stupid noodle that I have ever seen in my life.

MR. JOUR. (*to* NICOLE). Hold your tongue, will you? and mind your own business. I have wealth enough and to spare for my daughter. I only wish for honours, and I will have her a marchioness.

MRS. JOUR. A marchioness?

MR. JOUR. Yes, a marchioness.

MRS. JOUR. alas! God forbid.

MR. JOUR. It's a thing that I'm determined upon.

MRS. JOUR. I will never consent to it. Marriages between people who are not of the same rank are always subject to the most serious inconveniences. I do not wish to have a son-in-law who would have it in his power to reproach my daughter with her parentage; nor that she should have children who would be ashamed to call me their grandmother. If she came to see me with the equipage of a grand lady, and failed through inadvertency to salute some of the neighbours, people would not fail to say a thousand ill-natured things. "Just see," they would say, "our lady the marchioness, who is so puffed up now, she is Mr. Jourdain's daughter; she was only too pleased, when a child, to play at my lady with us. She has not always been so exalted as now, and her two grandfathers sold cloth near St. Innocents' Gate. They have laid a great deal of money by for their children, for which, may be, they are now paying dearly in the other world, for one does not generally become so rich by honest means." I do not wish to give occasion for such gossip, and I desire to meet with a man who, to cut it short, will be grateful to me for my daughter, and to whom I can say, "Sit down there, son-in-law, and dine with me."

MR. JOUR. How all these feelings show a narrow mind, satisfied to live for ever in a low condition of life. Let me have no more replies; my daughter shall be a marchioness in spite of everybody, and if you provoke me too much, I will make her a duchess.

SCENE XIII.—MRS. JOURDAIN, LUCILE, CLEONTE, NICOLE, COVIELLE.

MRS. JOUR. Do not give up all hope, Cleonte. Follow me, Lucile; come and tell your father with firmness and decision that, unless you have Cleonte for a husband, you will never marry.

SCENE XIV.—CLEONTE, COVIELLE.

COV. Well! you have done a fine piece of work, with your lofty sentiments.

CLE. What could I do? I have scruples on that subject which no precedent could overcome.

COV. What nonsense to be serious with a man like that! Do you not see that he is infatuated with one idea, and would it have cost you much to fall in with his gentility?

CLE. I am afraid you are right; but the fact is I had not thought before that it was necessary to show proofs of gentility in order to become Mr. Jourdain's son-in-law.

COV. (*laughing*). Ha! ha! ha!

CLE. What are you laughing at?

COV. At the thought of something that has just come into my head; it will play off our man, and help you to succeed in what you want.

CLE. How so?

COV. It is most amusing even to think of it.

CLE. What is it?

COV. We have had lately a certain masquerade, which seems to me the very thing wanted, and which I mean to make use of to play a trick on our absurd old fellow. The whole affair seems rather silly, but with him we may risk many things; there is no need of much cunning, and he is one to play his part wonderfully well, and to swallow greedily all the nonsense we may venture to tell him. I have actors and costumes all ready; only leave it to me.

CLE. But tell me....

COV. Yes, I must tell you all about it; but let us go away, for here he is coming back again.

SCENE XV.—MR. JOURDAIN (*alone*).

What the deuce does it all mean? They do nothing but reproach me with my great lords, and I, for my part, see nothing so fine as to associate with great lords; we find only honour and civility with them; and I would give two fingers of my hand to have been born a count or a marquis.

SCENE XVI.—MR. JOURDAIN, A SERVANT.

SER. Sir, here is the count, and a lady with him.

MR. JOUR. Bless me! and I have some orders to give. Tell them I shall be here in a moment.

SCENE XVII—DORIMENE, DORANTE, A SERVANT.

SER. My master says he will be here directly.

DOR. Very well.

SCENE XVIII.—DORIMENE, DORANTE.

DORI. I am afraid, Dorante, that I am doing a very strange thing in allowing myself to be brought by you into a house where I know nobody.

DOR. Where then can I go to entertain you, Madam, since, to avoid remarks being made, you will see me neither at your own house nor at mine?

DORI. Yes; but you do not mention that I am little by little brought to accept too great proofs of your love. In vain do I refuse my acquiescence in all you do, you triumph over my resistance, and you have a kind of persevering civility which causes me by degrees to do all that you wish. You began with frequent visits; next came declarations, and they have drawn after them serenades and entertainments, followed by presents. I was opposed to all these things, but you are not to be discouraged, and step by step you have overcome all my resolutions. For my part, I dare answer for nothing now; and I believe that at last you will persuade me to marry you, although I had set my heart against it.

DOR. Indeed, Madam, you should have been persuaded before. You are a widow, and depend on nobody but yourself. I am my own master, and I love you more than my life. What is there to prevent you from making me supremely happy?

DORI. To say the truth, Dorante, it requires many good qualities on both sides for people to live happily together, and the two most sensible people in the world will often find it difficult to make up a union with which they are satisfied.

DOR. You are wrong, Madam, to fear so many drawbacks to the happiness of a married life, and your sad experience proves nothing.

DORI. In short, I still come back to this; the expenses which you run into for my sake make me anxious for two reasons: the first that they involve me more than I should wish, and the other that I feel certain— pray be not offended with me—that you cannot incur them without much inconvenience to yourself; and I do not wish such a state of things to go on.

DOR. Ah, Madam, these are trifles not worth mentioning, and it is not from that....

DORI. I know what I am saying; and, among other things, the diamond you forced upon me is of a price....

DOR. Nay, Madam, do not set such value upon a thing which my love thinks so unworthy of you; and allow me.... Here is the master of the house.

SCENE XIX.—MR. JOURDAIN, DORIMENE, DORANTE.

MR. JOUR. (*after having made two bows, finds himself too near to* DORIMENE). A little farther, Madam.

DORI. What?

MR. JOUR. One step more, if you please.

DOR. What then?

MR. JOUR. Fall back a little for the third.

DOR. Mr. Jourdain, Madam, knows whom he is addressing.

MR. JOUR. Madam, it is a very great glory to me that I am fortunate enough to be so happy as to have the felicity that you should have had the goodness to do me the honour of honouring me with the favour of your presence, and had I also the merit to merit such merit as yours and that heaven ... envious of my good fortune ... had granted me ... the advantage of being worthy ... of the....

DOR. Mr. Jourdain, this is quite enough; Madam does not care for great compliments, and she knows that you are a clever and witty man. (*Aside to* DORIMENE) He is a harmless citizen, ridiculous enough, as you see, in his behaviour.

DORI. (*aside to* DORANTE). It is not difficult to perceive that.

DOR. Madam, this is one of my greatest friends.

MR. JOUR. You do me too much honour.

DOR. A most excellent and polite man.

DORI. I feel the greatest esteem for him.

MR. JOUR. I have done nothing as yet, Madam, to deserve such a favour.

DOR. (*aside to* MR. JOURDAIN). Be very careful not to speak to her of the diamond you gave her.

MR. JOUR (*aside to* DORANTE). May I not just ask her how she likes it?

DOR. (*aside to* MR. JOURDAIN). Eh? Be sure not to do that. It would be most vulgar of you; and to behave like a true gentleman, you should act in all things as if you had made no present at all. (*Aloud*) Mr. Jourdain says, Madam, that he is delighted to see you in his house.

DORI. He does me great honour.

MR. JOUR. (*aside to* DORANTE). How truly obliged I am to you, Sir, for speaking of me to her as you do.

DOR. (*aside to* MR. JOURDAIN). I had all the trouble in the world to make her come here.

MR. JOUR. (*as before*). I don't know how to thank you enough for it.

DOR. He says, Madam, that he thinks you the most beautiful woman in the world.

DORI. It is a great favour he does me.

MR. JOUR. Madam, it is you who grant the favours, and....

DOR. Let us think of the dinner.

SCENE XX.—MR. JOURDAIN, DORIMENE, DORANTE, A SERVANT.

SER. (*to* MR. JOURDAIN). Everything is ready, Sir.

DOR. Come, then, let us go and sit down. Tell the musicians to come.

SCENE XXI.—*Entry of the* BALLET.

The **COOKS,** *who have prepared the banquet, dance together, and make the third interlude; after which they bring in a table covered with various dishes.*

ACT IV.

SCENE I.—DORIMENE, MR. JOURDAIN, DORANTE, THREE SINGERS, A SERVANT.

DORI. Really, Dorante, this is a magnificent dinner.

MR. JOUR. You are pleased to say So, Madam, but I only wish it were more worthy of your acceptance.

(DORIMENE, MR. JOURDAIN, DORANTE, *and the* THREE SINGERS *sit down*.)

DOR. Mr. Jourdain is right, Madam, in what he says; and he obliges me by doing so well the honours of his house to you. I agree with him that the dinner is not worthy of you. As it was I who ordered it, and as I have not for this kind of thing the knowledge of some of our friends, you will not find here a well studied repast, but will meet with many incongruities of good eating and some barbarisms against good taste. If our good friend Damis had ordered it, all would be according to rule; there would be elegance and erudition everywhere; and he would not fail to exaggerate to you the excellence of every dish, and to make you acknowledge his high capacity in the science of good eating. He would speak to you of a loaf with golden sides, crusty all over, and yielding tenderly under the teeth; of wine full-bodied and of not too perceptible an acidity; of a saddle of mutton stewed with parsley; of a loin of Normandy veal, long, white, tender, and which is, as it were, an almond paste between the teeth; of partridges wonderful in flavour; and as his masterpiece, a pearl broth reinforced with a large turkey flanked with young pigeons, and crowned with white onions blended with endive. For my part I confess my ignorance; and as Mr. Jourdain has very well said, I wish the repast were more worthy of your acceptance.

DORI. Well, I can only answer to this compliment by eating as I am doing.

MR. JOUR. Ah! what beautiful hands!

DORI. The hands have not much to boast of, Mr. Jourdain; it is the diamond which you wish to speak of; it is indeed very beautiful.

MR. JOUR. I, Madam? Heaven forbid that I should speak of it. It would be ungentlemanly to do so, and the diamond is but a trifle.

DOR. You are difficult to please.

MR. JOUR. You are too kind, and....

DOR. (*after having made signs to* MR. JOURDAIN). Come, come, give a little wine to Mr. Jourdain and to these gentlemen, who will do us the pleasure of singing us a drinking song.

DORI. It is a most charming thought to make good music accompany good food, and I find myself most kindly entertained here.

The Shopkeeper Turned Gentleman

MR. JOUR. Madam, it is not....

DOR. Mr. Jourdain, let us listen to the music; what these gentlemen will tell us is better than all you and I could say.

1ST and **2ND SINGERS** *together, each with a glass in his hand*.

Phyllis, deign to fill my glass; Give the draught an added charm. Which is fairer, wine or lass, Love for both my heart doth arm?— In this hour supernal, Let us swear, while we can, For wine, woman, and man, A friendship eternal.

Ruby–red, the blushing wine, Paints thy lips with brighter shade, While its colours softer shine Where thy glances fall, fair maid!— While our youth is vernal, Let us swear, while we can, For wine, woman, and man, A friendship eternal.

Drinking Song.

Fill your glass, fill your glass, my friends, Let us drink, though time fly; We must live while we live, my friends, For time passes by.

When we cross the waves of the river, Wine and love say farewell We must leave them behind for ever, So value them well.

What though fools spend their time in thinking Of the true aim of life! Our philosophy lies in drinking, Not in wordy strife.

And glory, wisdom, and wealth, Do not ease life of ill, But we find our pleasure and health As the wine–cup we fill.

DORI. I never heard anything better sung, and all this is really beautiful.

MR. JOUR. I see something still more beautiful here, Madam.

DORI. Why, Mr. Jourdain, you are a greater flatterer than I should have thought.

DOR. And for what, Madam, do you take Mr. Jourdain?

The Shopkeeper Turned Gentleman

MR. JOUR. I wish she would take me for what I could name.

DORI. Again!

DOR. (*to* DORIMENE). You do not know him.

MR. JOUR. But she will know me whenever it pleases her.

DORI. Oh, I give up.

DOR. He is a man always ready with an answer. But do you not see, Madam, that Mr. Jourdain eats all the pieces you have touched.

DORI. Mr. Jourdain is a man I am charmed with.

MR. JOUR. If I could only charm your heart, I should be....

SCENE II.—MRS. JOURDAIN, MR. JOURDAIN, DORIMENE, DORANTE, SINGERS, SERVANTS.

MRS. JOUR. Ah! ah! I find charming company here, and I see clearly that I was not expected. It is for this fine piece of business, Sir, that you showed such anxiety to pack me off to my sister; was it? I have just seen a theatre down below, and here I find a banquet worthy of a wedding. That is the way you spend your money, and thus it is that you feast ladies in my absence, and give them music and the comedy, whilst you send me, trotting.

DOR. What do you mean, Mrs. Jourdain, and what fancies are you taking into your head to go and imagine that your husband is spending his money and giving the dinner to this lady? I beg to tell you that he has only lent me his house, and that it is I who give this feast, and not he. You should be a little more cautious in what you say.

MR. JOUR. Yes, rude woman that you are, it is the count who gives all that to this lady, who is a lady of rank. He does me the honour of making use of my house, and of wishing me to be with him.

MRS. JOUR. All this is rubbish; I know what I know.

DOR. Put on better spectacles, Mrs. Jourdain.

MRS. JOUR. I have no need of spectacles, Sir, and I see clearly enough what is going on. It is some time since I have seen things as they are, and I am no fool. It is very wrong of you, a great lord, to encourage my husband in his delusion. And for you, Madam, a great lady, it is neither handsome nor honest to sow dissension in a family, and to allow my husband to be in love with you.

DORI. What does all this mean? How very wrong of you, Dorante, to expose me to the preposterous fancies of this foolish woman.

DOR. (*following* DORIMENE, *who is going away*). Madam, stop, I pray; where are you going?

MR. JOUR. Madam.... My Lord the Count, present my humblest apologies to her and try to bring her back.

SCENE III.—MRS. JOURDAIN, MR. JOURDAIN, A SERVANT.

MR. JOUR. Ah! insolent woman that you are; these are your fine doings. You come and abuse me before everybody, and send away from my house persons of quality.

MRS. JOUR. I don't care a pin for their quality.

MR. JOUR. I don't know, accursed woman that you are, what prevents me from beating your skull in with what remains of the feast you have come and disturbed.

MRS. JOUR. (*going away*). I despise your threats. I come here to defend my own rights, and all wives will be on my side.

MR. JOUR. You do wisely to avoid my anger, I can tell you.

SCENE IV.—MR. JOURDAIN (*alone*).

She came in at a most unlucky moment. I was in a mood to tell her very pretty things, and I never felt so full of wit. But what does this mean?

SCENE V.—MR. JOURDAIN, COVIELLE (*disguised*).

COV. Sir, I am not sure if I have the honour of being known to you.

MR. JOUR. No, Sir.

COV. (*putting his hand about a foot from the ground*). I saw you when you were not taller than that.

MR. JOUR. Me?

COV. Yes! You were the most beautiful child in the world, and all the ladies used to lift you up in their arms to kiss you.

MR. JOUR. To kiss me?

COV. Yes. I was a great friend of the late nobleman your father.

MR. JOUR. Of the late nobleman my father?

COV. Yes, he was a most kind gentleman.

MR. JOUR. What do you say?

COV. I say that he was a most kind gentleman.

MR. JOUR. My father?

COV. Your father.

The Shopkeeper Turned Gentleman

MR. JOUR. You knew him well?

COV. Very well indeed.

MR. JOUR. And you know him to have been a nobleman?

COV. Undoubtedly.

MR. JOUR. Well, I don't understand what the world means.

COV. What do you say?

MR. JOUR. There are some stupid people who try to persuade me that he was a shopkeeper.

COV. He a shopkeeper! It is sheer calumny. All he did was this: he was extremely kind and obliging, and understood different kinds of stuff very well; therefore he used to go everywhere and choose some; then, he had them brought to his house, and was in the habit of letting his friends have some for money if they chose.

MR. JOUR. I am delighted to have made your acquaintance, so that you may testify that my father was a nobleman.

COV. I will maintain it before the whole world.

MR. JOUR. You will oblige me greatly; may I know what business brings you here?

COV. Since my acquaintance with your late father—a perfect gentleman, as I was telling you—I have travelled to the end of the world.

MR. JOUR. To the end of the world?

COV. Yes.

MR. JOUR. I suppose it is a very far-off country.

The Shopkeeper Turned Gentleman

COV. Very far off. I only returned four days ago, and owing to the interest I take in all that concerns you, I have come to give you the best news possible.

MR. JOUR. What can it be?

COV. You know that the son of the Grand Turk is here. [Footnote: There seems to have been a Turkish envoy in Paris at that time.]

MR. JOUR. No, I didn't know.

COV. You didn't know! He has a most magnificent retinue of attendants. Everybody goes to see him, and he has been received in this country as a personage of the greatest importance.

MR. JOUR. Indeed? I have heard nothing of it.

COV. What is of great concern to you is that he is in love with your daughter.

MR. JOUR. The son of the Grand Turk?

COV. Yes, and that he wishes to, become your son-in-law.

MR. JOUR. My son-in-law, the son of the Grand Turk!

COV. The son of the Grand Turk your son-in-law When I went to see him, as I understand his language perfectly, we had a long chat together; and after having talked of different things, he told me, *Acciam croc soler onch alla moustaph gidelum amanahem varahini oussere carbulath*? that is to say, "Have you not seen a beautiful young girl who is the daughter of Mr. Jourdain, a nobleman of Paris?"

MR. JOUR. The son of the Grand Turk said that of me?

COV. Yes. Then I answered him that I knew you perfectly well, and that I had seen your daughter. Ah! said he, *marababa sahem*! which is to say, "Ah! how much I love her!"

MR. JOUR. *Marababa sahem*! means, "Ah! how I love her!"

The Shopkeeper Turned Gentleman

COV. Yes.

MR. JOUR. Indeed, you do right to tell me; for I should never have known that *Marababa sahem*! meant, "Ah I how much I love her!" This Turkish language is admirable.

COV. More admirable than you would ever imagine. For instance, do you know what *Cacaracamouchen* means?

MR. JOUR. *Cacaracamouchen*? No.

COV. It means, "My dear love."

MR. JOUR. *Cacaracamouchen* means, "My dear love"?

COV. Yes.

MR. JOUR. It is wonderful! *Cacaracamouchen*, "My dear love." Who would ever have thought it? I am perfectly astounded.

COV. In short, in order to end my embassy, I must tell you that he is coming to ask your daughter in marriage; and in order to have a father-in-law worthy of him, he wants to make you a *mamamouchi*, which is a great dignity in his country.

MR. JOUR. *Mamamouchi*?

COV. *Mamamouchi*; that is to say in our own language, a paladin. Paladin, you know those ancient paladins; in short, there is nothing more noble than that in the whole world, and you will take rank with the greatest lords upon the earth.

MR. JOUR. The son of the Grand Turk honours me greatly, and I beg of you to take me to his house, that I may return him my thanks.

COV. Not at all; he is just coming here.

MR. JOUR. He is coming here?

COV. Yes, and he is bringing with him everything necessary for the ceremony.

MR. JOUR. It is doing things rather quickly.

COV. Yes, his love will suffer no delay.

MR. JOUR. All that perplexes me in this affair is that my daughter is a very obstinate girl, who has taken it into her head to have a certain Cleonte for her husband, and vows she will marry no other.

COV. She is sure to change her mind when she sees the son of the Grand Turk; besides, wonderful to relate, the son of the Grand Turk has a strong likeness to that very Cleonte. People showed him to me, and I have just seen him; the love she feels for the one is sure to pass to the other, and ... I hear him coming! Lo, here he is.

SCENE VI.—CLEONTE (*dressed as a Turk*), THREE PAGES (*carrying the vest of* CLEONTE), MR. JOURDAIN, COVIELLE.

CLE. *Ambousahim oqui boraf, Giourdina, salamatequi.*

COV. (*to* MR. JOURDAIN). That is to say, "Mr. Jourdain, may your heart be all the year round a budding rose tree." It is a way of speaking they have in that country.

MR. JOUR. I am your Turkish highness's humble servant.

COV. *Carigar camboto oustin moraf.*

CLE. *Oustin yoc catamalequi basum base alla moran.*

COV. He says, "May heaven grant you the strength of the lion and the prudence of the serpent."

MR. JOUR. His Turkish highness does me too much honour, and I wish him all manner of prosperity.

The Shopkeeper Turned Gentleman

COV. *Ossa binamen sadoc baballi oracaf ouram.*

CLE. *Belmen.*

COV. He says you must go quickly with him to prepare for the ceremony, in order afterwards to see your daughter and conclude the marriage.

MR. JOUR. So many things comprised in two words?

COV. Yes, The Turkish language is like that, it says a good deal in a few words. Go quickly where he wishes you.

SCENE VII.—COVIELLE (*alone*).

Ah! ah! ah! Upon my soul, this is most absurd. What a dupe! Had he learnt his part by heart, he would not have played it better. Ah! ah! ah!

SCENE VIII.—DORANTE, COVIELLE.

COV. I beg of you, Sir, to help us here in a little affair we have in hand.

DOR. Hallo! Covielle, who would have known you again? What a get up!

COV. As you see. Ah! ah! ah!

DOR. What are you laughing at?

COV. At a thing worth laughing at, I can tell you.

DOR. What is it?

COV. You would never guess the stratagem we have invented to induce Mr. Jourdain to give my master his daughter in marriage.

DOR. I certainly can't guess what it is, but I can guess that it will succeed since you are at the head of affairs.

COV. I know, Sir, that the animal is appreciated by you.

DOR. Tell me what you are about.

COV. Kindly go a little on one side to make room for what I see coming. You will be able to have a view of a part of the business whilst I explain the rest to you.

SCENE IX.—THE TURKISH CEREMONY. [Footnote: Lulli composed the music, and acted the part of the Mufti.]

THE MUFTI, DERVISHES, TURKS (*assisting the* MUFTI), **SINGERS** and **DANCERS**.

SIX TURKS *enter gravely, two and two at the sound of instruments*. They carry three carpets which they lift very high as they dance several dances The TURKS *pass under the carpets, singing and range themselves on each side of the stage. The* MUFTI, *accompanied by* DERVISHES, *closes the march. The* TURKS *then spread the carpets on the ground, and kneel down upon them. The* MUFTI *and the* DERVISHES *stand up in the middle of them; and while the* MUFTI *invokes Mahomet in dumb contortions and grimaces the* TURKS *prostrate themselves to the ground, singing* Alli, *raising their hands to heaven, singing* Alla, *and continue so alternately to the end of the invocation; after which they all rise up, singing,* Alla eckber, *and two* DERVISHES *go and fetch* MR. JOURDAIN.

SCENE X.—THE MUFTI, DERVISH, TURKISH SINGERS *and* DANCERS. MR. JOURDAIN, *dressed like a Turk, his head shaved, without any turban or sword*.

THE MUFTI (*to* MR. JOURDAIN).

[1] Se ti sabir, Ti respondir; Se non sabir, Tazir, tazir.

Mi star muphti, Ti qui star si? Non intendir; Tazir, tazir. [2]

[1] *Lingua franca,* jargon composed of Italian, Spanish, and spoken in the Levant.

[2] If you understand, Answer; If you do not understand, Hold thy peace, hold thy peace. I am the Mufti

(TWO DERVISHES *retire with* MR. JOURDAIN.)

SCENE XI.—THE MUFTI, DERVISHES, TURKS, *singing and dancing*.

MUF. Dice, Turque, qui star quista? Anabatista? anabatista? [Say, Turk, who is this? Is he Anabaptist? Anabaptist?]

TUR. Ioc. [No.]

MUF. Zuinglista? [A Zwinglian?]

TUR. Ioc. [No.]

MUF. Coffita? [A Capht?]

TUR. Ioc. [No.]

MUF. Hussita? Morista? Fronista? [A Hussite? a Moor? a Phronist?]

TUR. Ioc, ioc; ioc. [No, no, no.]

MUF. Ioc, ioc, ioc. Star pagana? [No, no, no. Is he a pagan?]

TUR. Ioc. [No.]

MUF. Luterana? [A Lutheran?]

The Shopkeeper Turned Gentleman

TUR. Ioc. [No.]

MUF. Puritana? [A Puritan?]

TUR. Ioc. [No.]

MUF. Bramina? Moffina? Zurina? [A Brahmin? a Moffian? a Zurian?]

TUR. Ioc, ioc, ioc. [No, no, no.]

MUF. Ioc, ioc, ioc. Mahametana? Mahametana? [No, no, no. A Mahometan? a Mahometan?]

TUR. Hi Valla. Hi Valla. [There you have it. There you have it.]

MUF. Como chamara? Como chamara? [How is he called? How is he called?]

TUR. Giourdina, Giourdina. [Jourdain, Jourdain.]

MUF. (*jumping*). Giourdina, Giourdina. [Jourdain, Jourdain.]

TUR. Giourdina, Giourdina. [Jourdain, Jourdain.]

THE MUFTI. [1]

Mahameta, per Giourdina, Mi pregar sera e matina. Voler far un paladina De Giourdina, de Giourdina; Dar turbanta, e dar scarrina, Con galera, e brigantina, Per deffender Palestina. Mahameta, per Giourdina, Mi pregar sera e matina. (*To the* TURKS.) Star bon Turca Giourdina?

[1] To Mahomet for Jourdain, I pray night and day. I wish to make a paladin Of Jourdain, of Jourdain. Give him a turban, and give him a sword, With a galley and a brigantine, To defend Palestine. To Mahomet for Jourdain I pray night and day. (*To the* TURKS.). Is Jourdain a good Turk?

TUR. Hi Valla. Hi Valla. [Yes, by Allah!]

MUF. (*singing and dancing*). Ha la ba, ba la chou, ba la ba, ba la da.

TUR. Ha la ba, ba la chou, ba la ba ba la da. [2]

[2] Thus separated, these words have no sense; but by joining and correcting them, we have: *Allah baba, hou, Allah hou,* which are really Turkish, and which signify, "*God my Father; God my Father.*" (Auger.)

SCENE XI.—TURKS, *singing and dancing. Second entry of the* BALLET.

SCENE XIII.—THE MUFTI, DERVISHES, MR. JOURDAIN, TURKS, *singing and dancing*.

The MUFTI *returns, wearing on his head the state turban, which is of enormous size, and adorned with lighted candles, four or five rows deep; he is accompanied by* TWO DERVISHES *bearing the Koran, and wearing cone-shaped caps also adorned with lighted candles.*

The two other **DERVISHES** *lead in* **MR. JOURDAIN,** *and make him kneel down, his two hands on the ground, so that his back, on which the Koran is placed, serves for a desk for the* MUFTI, *who makes a second burlesque invocation, knitting his eyebrows, striking from time to time on the Koran, and turning over the pages with precipitation; after which, lifting up his hands, he cries with a loud voice,* "**HOU.**"

During this second invocation, the other TURKS, *bowing down and raising themselves alternately, sing likewise,* "**Hou, hou, hou.**"

MR. JOUR. (*after they have taken the Koran from off his back*). Ouf!

THE MUFTI (*to* MR. JOURDAIN). Ti non star furba? [Thou wilt not be a knave?]

THE TURKS. No, no, no.

THE MUFTI. Non star forfanta? [Nor be a thief?]

The Shopkeeper Turned Gentleman

THE TURKS. No, no, no.

THE MUFTI (*to the* TURKS). Donar turbanta. [Give the turban.]

THE TURKS. Ti non star furba? [Thou wilt not be a knave?] No, no, no. Non star forfanta? [Nor be a thief?] No, no, no. Donar turbanta. [Give the turban.]

Third entry of the BALLET.

The **TURKS**, *dancing, put the turban on* **MR. JOURDAIN'S** *head at the sound of the instruments*.

THE MUFTI (*giving a sabre to* MR. JOURDAIN). Ti star nobile, non star fabbola. [Be brave, be no Scoundrel] Pigliar schiabbola [Take the Sword.]

THE TURKS (*drawing their sabres*). Ti star nobile, non star fabbola. [Be brave, be no Scoundrel] Pigliar schiabbola. [Take the Sword.]

Fourth entry of the **BALLET**.

The **TURKS**, *dancing, strike* **MR. JOURDAIN** *several times with their swords, keeping time with the music*.

THE MUFTI. Dara, dara Bastonnara. [Give, give the bastonnade.]

THE TURKS. Dara, dara Bastonnara. [Give, give the bastonnade.]

Fifth entry of the **BALLET**.

The **Turks**, *dancing, give* **MR. JOURDAIN** *several blows with a stick, keeping time meanwhile*.

THE MUFTI. Non tener honta; [Think it not a shame;] Questa star l'ultima affronta. [This is the last affront.]

THE TURKS. Non tener honta; [Think it not a shame;] Questa star l'ultima affronta. [This is the last affront.]

The **MUFTI** *begins a third invocation.* The DERVISHES *support him under the arms with great respect, after which the* TURKS, *singing and dancing round the* MUFTI, *retire with him, and lead off* MR. JOURDAIN.

ACT V.

SCENE I.—MRS. JOURDAIN, MR. JOURDAIN.

MRS. JOUR. Goodness gracious me! Lord, have mercy on us! What can this be? What a figure! Is it a *momon* [Footnote: Apparently there is no English equivalent to *momon* in this sense.] you have in hand, and is this carnival time? Do speak! What does all this mean? Who trussed you up in this manner?

MR. JOUR. Just see the impertinent woman, to speak after such a manner to a *mamamouchi*.

MRS. JOUR. What do you say?

MR. JOUR. Yes, you must show me respect now; I have just been made a *mamamouchi*.

MRS. JOUR. What can you possibly mean with your *mamamouchi*?

MR. JOUR. *Mamamouchi*, I tell you; I am a *mamamouchi*.

MRS. JOUR. What kind of a beast is that?

MR. JOUR. *Mamamouchi*; which in our language means paladin.

MRS. JOUR. Ballet in? Are you of an age to be dancing ballets?

MR. JOUR. What an ignorant woman you are! I say "paladin," which is a dignity which has just been conferred upon me with all due ceremony.

The Shopkeeper Turned Gentleman

MRS. JOUR. What ceremony?

MR. JOUR. *Mahameta per Jordina.*

MRS. JOUR. What does that mean?

MR. JOUR. *Jordina, that is to say Jourdain.*

MRS. JOUR. Well? What, Jourdain?

MR. JOUR. *Voler far un paladina de Jordina.*

MRS. JOUR. What?

MR. JOUR. *Dar turbanta con galera.*

MRS. JOUR. What does that mean?

MR. JOUR. *Per deffender Palestina.*

MRS. JOUR. Tell me what you mean then.

MR. JOUR. *Dara, dara bastonnara.*

MRS. JOUR. What is all this jargon?

MR. JOUR. *Non tener honta, questa star l'ultima affronta.*

MRS. JOUR. Whatever is all this?

MR. JOUR. (*singing and dancing*). *Hou la ba, ba la chow, ba la ba, ba la da.* (*Falls to the ground.*)

MRS. JOUR. Alas, alas! my husband is gone out of his mind.

MR. JOUR. (*getting up and walking off*). Peace! Show respect to the *mamamouchi*.

The Shopkeeper Turned Gentleman

MRS. JOUR. (*alone*). Where can he have lost his senses? I must run after him and prevent him from going out! (*Seeing* DORIMENE *and* DORANTE.) Oh dear! Oh dear! Here's the last straw! I see nothing but trouble and disgrace everywhere!

SCENE II.—DORANTE, DORIMENE.

DOR. Yes, Madam, it is the most amusing thing that you ever saw, and I do not think that there is in the whole world a man as, crazy as this one. Moreover, we must try to help Cleonte and back up his masquerade. He is a most excellent fellow, and one who deserves all your interest.

DORI. I have the greatest esteem for him, and he is worthy of all success.

DOR. We also have here, Madam, a ballet due to us. We must not miss it, for I should be glad to see if my idea succeeds.

DORI. I saw magnificent preparations yonder; and this is a state of things, Dorante, with which I can bear no longer. Yes, I must put an end to your profusion; and in order to cut short all the expenses I see you run into for me, I have decided upon marrying you as soon as possible. This is the real secret of my decision; all these things, as you know, end ever in matrimony.

DOR. Ah, Madam, is it possible that you should have come to such a kind determination in my favour?

DORI. It is only to prevent you from ruining yourself, for, if I am not quick, I clearly see that before long you will not have a penny left.

DOR. What thanks I owe you for your anxiety about my fortune! That and my heart are entirely yours, and you can dispose of both as shall seem good to you.

DORI. I will make a right use of both. But here is our man coming. What an admirable figure!

SCENE III.—MR. JOURDAIN, DORIMENE, DORANTE.

DOR. Sir, we have both come to do homage to your new dignity, and to rejoice with you over the marriage of your daughter with the son of the Grand Turk.

MR. JOUR. (*after bowing in the Turkish manner*). Sir, I wish you the strength of the serpent, and the wisdom of the lion.

DORI. I am very glad to be one of the first, Sir, to come and congratulate you on the high degree of glory to which you are raised.

MR. JOUR. Madam, may your rose-tree bloom all the year round. I am infinitely obliged to you for interesting yourself in the honour just bestowed upon me; and I am greatly rejoiced to see you back here, so that I may tender to you my most humble apologies for the extraordinary conduct of my wife.

DORI. Don't speak about it. I excuse in her such a momentary impulse; your heart ought to be very precious to her; and it is not to be wondered at that the possession of such a man as you are may cause her some alarm.

MR. JOUR. The possession of my heart is a thing you have altogether acquired.

DOR. You see, Madam, that Mr. Jourdain is not one of those whom prosperity blinds, and that, even in his elevation, he knows how to recognise his friends.

DORI. It is the proof of a truly generous soul.

DOR. Where can his Turkish highness be? We should like, as your friends, to pay our homage to him.

MR. JOUR. Here he is coming, and I sent for my daughter to give him her hand.

SCENE IV.—MR. JOURDAIN, DORIMENE, DORANTE, CLEONTE (*dressed as a Turk*).

DORI. (*to* CLEONTE). Sir, we come, as friends of your father-in-law, to salute your highness, and to assure you with all respect of our most humble services.

MR. JOUR. Where is the interpreter, to tell him who you are, and to make him understand what you say? You shall see that he will answer you, and he speaks Turkish wonderfully well. Holla, here! where the deuce is he gone? (*To* CLEONTE) *Strouf strif, strof, straf.* This gentleman is a *grande segnore, grande segnore, grande segnore* ; and this lady a *granda dama, granda dama. (Seeing that he is not understood)* Ah! *(To* CLEONTE, *showing him* DORANTE*)* This gentleman is a French mamamouchi, and the lady she is a French mamamouchess. I cannot explain myself more clearly. Good! Here is the interpreter.

SCENE V.—MR. JOURDAIN, DORIMENE, DORANTE, CLEONTE (*dressed as a Turk*); COVIELLE (*disguised*).

MR. JOUR. Where are you going, then? You know that we can say nothing without you. (*Showing* CLEONTE.) Just tell him that this gentleman and this lady are people of very high rank, who have come to pay their homage to him, as friends of mine, and to assure him of their services. (*To* DORIMENE *and* DORANTE) You will see how he will answer.

COV. *Alabala crociam acci boram alabamen.*

CLE. *Catalequi tubal ouria soter amalouchan.*

MR. JOUR. (to DORIMENE and DORANTE). Do you see?

COV. He says, "May the rain of prosperity water at all times the garden of your family."

MR. JOUR. I told you that he spoke Turkish.

DOR. This is admirable.

SCENE VI.—LUCILE, CLEONTE, MR. JOURDAIN, DORIMENE, DORANTE, COVIELLE.

MR. JOUR. Come, my daughter; come near, and give your hand to this gentleman, who does you the honour of asking you in marriage.

LUC. Why, father, how strangely dressed you are! Are you acting a comedy?

MR. JOUR. No, no; it is no comedy, but a very serious affair, and the most honourable for you that could ever be wished for. (*Showing* CLEONTE.) Here is the husband I bestow upon you.

LUC. Bestow upon me, father?

MR. JOUR. Yes, upon you. There, give him your hand, and thank heaven for your good fortune.

LUC. I have no wish to marry.

MR. JOUR. It is all very well, but I wish it; I who am your father.

LUC. I will do nothing of the kind.

MR. JOUR. Ah! what a noise! Come, I say, give him your hand.

LUC. No, father; I told you already that no power upon earth will force me to marry any other but Cleonte; and I would have recourse to any extremity rather than.... (*Recognising* CLEONTE.) But it is true that you are my father, and that I owe you absolute obedience; dispose of me, then, according to your will.

MR. JOUR. Truly, I am delighted to see you return so quickly to a sense of your duty; and it is a pleasure to me to have such an obedient daughter.

SCENE VII.—MRS. JOURDAIN. CLEONTE, MR. JOURDAIN, LUCILE, DORANTE, DORIMENE, COVIELLE.

MRS JOUR. What is it? What is the meaning of all this? They say you want to give your daughter in marriage to a mummer.

MR. JOUR. Will you be silent? You always come and disturb everything with your follies; and there is no possibility of teaching you how to behave yourself.

MRS. JOUR. It is because there is no possibility of making you wise; and you go from folly to folly. What are your intentions? and what do you mean to do with all this assembly of people?

MR. JOUR. I wish to marry my daughter to the son of the Grand Turk.

MRS. JOUR. To the son of the Grand Turk?

MR. JOUR. (*showing* COVIELLE). Yes; ask the interpreter to present your compliments to him from you.

MRS. JOUR. I have no need of an interpreter, and I can tell him myself easily to his face that he shall not have my daughter.

MR. JOUR. Will you be silent? I ask once more.

DOR. What! Mrs. Jourdain, you oppose yourself to such an honour as this? You refuse his Turkish highness for a son-in-law?

MRS. JOUR. Good gracious, Sir! Mind your own business, if you please.

DORI. It is an honour by no means to be rejected.

MRS. JOUR. I pray you also not to trouble yourself with that which is no concern of yours.

DOR. It is the friendship we have for you which makes us interest ourselves in your welfare.

MRS. JOUR. I can do very well without your friendship.

DOR. You see that your daughter yields to her father's will.

MRS. JOUR. My daughter consents to marry a Turk?

DOR. Certainly.

MRS. JOUR. She can forget Cleonte?

DOR. What will not one do to be a grand lady?

MRS. JOUR. I would strangle her with my own hands if she had done such a thing.

MR. JOUR. Too much prating by half! I tell you the marriage shall take place.

MRS. JOUR. And I tell you that it shan't.

MR. JOUR. Ah! what a row!

LUC. Mother!

MRS. JOUR. Leave me alone, you are a bad girl.

MR. JOUR. (*to* MRS. JOURDAIN). What! you scold her because she is obedient to me?

MRS. JOUR. Certainly; she belongs to me as much as she belongs to you.

COV. (*to* MRS. JOURDAIN). Madam.

MRS. JOUR. What business have you to speak to me, you?

COV. One word.

The Shopkeeper Turned Gentleman

MRS. JOUR. I'll have nothing to do with your word.

COV. (*to* MR. JOURDAIN). Sir, if she will only listen to a word in private, I promise you to make her consent to all you want.

MRS. JOUR. I will never consent to it.

COV. Only hear me.

MRS. JOUR. No.

MR. JOUR. (*to* MRS. JOURDAIN). Hear him.

MRS. JOUR. No; I will not hear him.

MR. JOUR. He will tell you....

MRS. JOUR. I don't want him to tell me anything.

MR. JOUR. Did ever anybody see such obstinacy in a woman! Would it hurt you to hear him?

COV. Only listen to me; you may do what you please afterwards.

MRS. JOUR. Well, what?

COV. (*aside, to* MRS. JOURDAIN). We have made signs to you for the last hour. Do you not see that all this is done to fit in with the fancies of your husband? that we are imposing upon him under this disguise, and that it is Cleonte himself who is the son of the Grand Turk?

MRS. JOUR. (*aside, to* COVIELLE). Oh! oh!

COV. (*aside, to* MRS. JOURDAIN). And that it is I, Covielle, who am the interpreter?

MRS. JOUR. (*aside, to* COVIELLE). Ah! if it is so, I give in.

COV. (*aside, to* MRS. JOURDAIN). Seem not to have any idea of what's going on.

MRS. JOUR. (*aloud*). Very well, let it be; I consent to the marriage.

MR. JOUR. So, everyone is agreed. (*To* MRS. JOURDAIN) You would not listen to him. I knew he would explain to you what the son of the Grand Turk is.

MRS. JOUR. He has explained it quite sufficiently, and I am satisfied with it. Let us send for a notary.

DOR. The very thing! And Mrs. Jourdain, in order to set your mind at rest, and that you should lose to–day all feelings of jealousy which you may have felt about your husband, this lady and I will ask the same notary to marry us.

MRS. JOUR. I consent to that also.

MR. JOUR. (*aside*, to DORANTE). It is to deceive her, is it not?

DOR. (*aside*, to MR. JOURDAIN). We must amuse her with this notion.

MR. JOUR. Good, good. (*Aloud*) Let somebody go at once for the notary.

DOR. Whilst he draws up the contract, let us see our ballet, and give the entertainment to his Turkish highness.

MR. JOUR. It is well thought of. Let us go to our places.

MRS. JOUR. And Nicole?

MR. JOUR. I give her to the interpreter, and my wife to anyone who will have her.

COV. Sir, I thank you. (*Aside*) If it is possible to find a greater fool than this one, I will go and publish it in Rome.

BALLET AND DIVERTISSEMENT.

CPSIA information can be obtained
at www.ICGtesting.com
Printed in the USA
LVOW09s0819060618
579778LV00011B/317/P